VIDEO COURSE

TOP NOTCH TV

Joan Saslow ■ Allen Ascher

with *Top Notch Pop Songs and Karaoke*
by Rob Morsberger

PEARSON
Longman

**Top Notch TV 3
Video Course**

Copyright © 2008 by Pearson Education, Inc.
All rights reserved.

No part of this publication may be reproduced, stored
in a retrieval system, or transmitted in any form or
by any means, electronic, mechanical, photocopying,
recording, or otherwise, without the prior permission of the publisher.

Pearson Education, 10 Bank Street, White Plains, NY 10606

Staff credits: The people who made up the *Top Notch TV 3 Video Course* team—representing editorial, production, design, and manufacturing—are Rhea Banker, Dave Dickey, Pamela Fishman, Aliza Greenblatt, Ray Keating, Mike Kemper, Katherine Keyes, Jessica Miller-Smith, and Mike Mone.

Text composition: TSI Graphics

Text font: Utopia

Illustration credits: Steve Attoe, pp. 22, 82; Mark Collins, p. 62; Brian Hughes, pp. 23, 45, 46; Andy Myer, p. 77; Dusan Petric, p. 13.

Photo credits: All photos unless noted below are from the *Top Notch TV* Video Program. David Mager, p. 9; Shutterstock, p. 19 (bottom); p. 23 (copier) Xerox Corporation; (dry cleaner) bikeriderlondon/Shutterstock, (tailor) David Mager, Stewart Cohen/Getty Images (caterer); p. 27, photos courtesy of Stephanie Biernbaum, Lordan Napoli, and Larry Jay Tish; p. 33 Benelux Press/Index Stock Imagery; p. 41 (fireworks) SuperStock, (parades) Chip East/Corbis, (picnics) Vasiliy Koval/Fotolia, (pray) Zafer Kizilkaya/Coral Planet, (gifts) Ryan McVay/Getty Images, (dead) Doug Martin/Photo Researchers, Inc., (costumes) Philip Gould/Corbis; p. 84 (shark) Shutterstock.com, (scorpion) Shutterstock.com; p. 89 (snake) Shutterstock.com, (mosquito) Timothy Fadek/Corbis Sygma, (jellyfish) Shutterstock.com.

ISBN 13: 978-0-13-205863-6
ISBN 10: 0-13-205863-4

Printed in the United States of America
5 6 7 8 9 10—V082—16 15 14

Contents

Scope and sequence of content and skills iv
About the Video Course vi
About the authors vii
Meet the *Top Notch TV* stars viii
Meet the on-the-street interviewees ix

UNIT 1   I'm a little early, aren't I? 1
    Scene 1 2
    Scene 2 4
    Top Notch Pop song: *It's a Great Day for Love* 8

UNIT 2   Are you OK? 9
    Scene 1 11
    Scene 2 15
    Interviews: *Are you traditional in your medical ideas?* 17

UNIT 3   I need to get a package to Australia a.s.a.p.! 19
    Scene 1 21
    Scene 2 24
    Top Notch Pop song: *I'll Get Back to You* 26

UNIT 4   I could have been a great dancer. 27
    Scene 1 28
    Scene 2 30
    Interviews: *How would you describe your skills and abilities?* 33

UNIT 5   I want a large wedding. 35
    Scene 1 36
    Scene 2 39
    Interviews: *Could you please describe a typical wedding in your country?* ... 42
    Top Notch Pop song: *Endless Holiday* 44

UNIT 6   I want to go someplace different. 45
    Scene 1 46
    Scene 2 49
    Top Notch Pop song: *Lucky to Be Alive* 53

UNIT 7   May I ask you what you're reading? 54
    Scene 1 57
    Scene 2 59
    Interviews: *Do you do a lot of reading?* 61

UNIT 8   Technology today is amazing! 64
    Scene 1 66
    Scene 2 69
    Top Notch Pop song: *Reinvent the Wheel* 71

UNIT 9   Can we please avoid discussing politics? 72
    Scene 1 74
    Scene 2 76
    Interviews: *How do you feel about...?* 79

UNIT 10   We weren't going to tell you this, but... 82
    Scene 1 84
    Scene 2 88

Video scripts 91
Lyrics for *Top Notch Pop* songs 102
Answer key 106

Scope and sequence of content and skills

UNIT	Social Language	Vocabulary	Grammar
1 I'm a little early, aren't I? *Page 1*	• Make small talk • Ask how someone would like to be addressed • Explain customs	• Ways to discuss proper address • Manners and etiquette	• Tag questions • The past perfect
2 Are you OK? *Page 9*	• Describe symptoms • Show concern	• Medical treatments and medications • Symptoms	• *May, might, must* • *Be able to*
3 I need to get a package to Australia, a.s.a.p.! *Page 19*	• Request express service • Recommend a service provider • Plan a social event	• Services • Service providers • Adjectives to describe services	• The passive causative • Causatives *get, have,* and *make* • *Let*
4 I could have been a great dancer. *Page 27*	• Explain life choices • Express regrets	• Skills and abilities	• The future in the past • Perfect modals
5 I want a large wedding. *Page 35*	• Discuss a wedding • Discuss holiday traditions	• Getting married • Ways to describe a holiday • Ways to commemorate a holiday	• Adjective clauses with subject relative pronouns • Adjective clauses with object relative pronouns

UNIT	Social Language	Vocabulary	Grammar
6 **I want to go someplace different.** *Page 45*	• Express fear of disasters • Reassure someone • Convey a message	• Natural disasters and other emergencies	• Direct and indirect speech
7 **May I ask you what you're reading?** *Page 54*	• Agree to lend someone something • Describe reading material	• Types of books • Ways to describe a book • Some ways to enjoy reading	• Noun clauses: embedded questions • Noun clauses as direct objects
8 **Technology today is amazing!** *Page 64*	• Describe innovative products • Offer advice	• Ways to describe inventions and manufactured products	• Factual and unreal conditional sentences
9 **Can we please avoid discussing politics?** *Page 72*	• State an opinion • Disagree politely about controversial issues • Discuss politics	• Global issues • A continuum of political and social beliefs • Ways to agree and disagree • Some controversial issues • Ways to express opinions	• Non-count nouns for abstract ideas • Verbs followed by objects and infinitives
10 **We weren't going to tell you this, but . . .** *Page 82*	• Warn about risks and dangers • Describe the natural world	• Geographical features • Possible risks • Positive and negative comments about places • Dangerous animals and insects	• Infinitives with *too* + an adjective

About the Video Course

The *Top Notch TV Video Course* consists of four *Top Notch TV* videos and their corresponding Video Course Books. The course can be used in a number of ways:

- As a stand-alone video-based listening / speaking course that teaches key vocabulary, grammar, and social language
- As a video-plus-workbook supplement to accompany the *Top Notch* course*
- As a video-plus-workbook complement to any low-beginning to intermediate level English language course
- As a self-study or distance learning video-plus-workbook program

Top Notch TV

Top Notch TV consists of four graded videos designed for English language learning, ranging from true-beginner level to high-intermediate level. The videos contain:

- A hilarious TV-style sitcom (with a TV-style laugh track)
- Authentic, unrehearsed on-the-street interviews of speakers with a variety of accents
- Original *Top Notch Pop* songs and karaoke
- Optional closed captioning

Scope and sequence

The scope and sequence chart on pages iv–v provides the language focus of each of the ten units of this Video Course Book. Answers to exercises and complete video scripts and *Top Notch Pop* song lyrics can be found at the end of this book.

Unit organization

Each unit begins with a **Preview** section which presents and practices key language that will occur in the video. Then activities for each video segment are organized into two sections: **View** and **Extend**.

View activities focus on comprehension and include "Sneak peeks" to build expectation for the topics of the sitcom episodes. **View** sections also include "Language in use" boxes pointing out interesting facts about spoken English.

Extend sections present additional topically related vocabulary and useful grammar to boost students' oral and written fluency. **Extend** activities have been designed either for self-study or for classroom interaction. They include opportunities for writing practice as well as "Speaking options" for pair and group discussion.

A *Top Notch Pop* song section includes activities that practice the target language included in the *Top Notch Pop* song.

Note: Video Scripts, Lyrics, and Answer Keys are perforated and can be removed.

---

*Top Notch is a complete four-level communicative course for adults and young adults. Together with *Summit 1* and *2*, it forms a six-level course with a full range of print and multimedia materials, including *Top Notch TV* and *Summit TV*.

About the authors

Joan Saslow

Ms. Saslow is co-author with Allen Ascher of the six-level award-winning adult course *Top Notch* and *Summit*. She was the series director of *True Colors*.

Joan Saslow is also author of a number of additional multilevel courses for adults: *Ready to Go*, *Workplace Plus*, and *Literacy Plus*, and of *English in Context: Reading Comprehension for Science and Technology*.

Ms. Saslow taught in Chile at the Binational Centers of Valparaíso and Viña del Mar and at the Catholic University of Valparaíso. In the United States, Ms. Saslow taught English as a Foreign Language to Japanese university students at Marymount College and to international students in Westchester Community College's intensive English program. She also taught workplace English at General Motors. She is a frequent speaker at gatherings of English teachers throughout the world. Ms. Saslow has an M.A. in French from the University of Wisconsin.

Allen Ascher

Allen Ascher, co-author with Joan Saslow of the six-level award-winning adult course *Top Notch* and *Summit*, is the author of the popular *Think about Editing: A Grammar Editing Guide for ESL Writers*. Mr. Ascher played a key publishing role in the creation of some of the most widely used materials for adults, including: *True Colors*, *NorthStar*, *Focus on Grammar*, *Global Links*, and *Ready to Go*.

Mr. Ascher has been a teacher and teacher-trainer in both China and the United States and was Academic Director of the International English Language Institute at Hunter College. He taught all skills and levels at the City University of New York and trained teachers in the certificate program at the New School. He has provided lively workshops at conferences throughout Asia, Latin America, North America, Europe, and the Middle East. Mr. Ascher has an M.A. in Applied Linguistics from Ohio University.

Meet the Top Notch TV stars

Mr. Evans, president of the Top Notch Travel Agency

Bob, a travel agent

Cheryl, the office manager

Paul, a tour guide

Marie, the receptionist

Meet the on-the-street interviewees

(Any accents that depart from non-regional American English are labeled.)

Alvino

Blanche / Herb

Christiane
(Austria)

Dan

Emma

Ian

James
(U.S. South)

Jessica
(Germany)

Joe

Lisa

Lorayn

Matt
(U.S. Boston)

Rita
(U.S. New York City)

San

Stephan
(Greece)

Vanessa
(U.S. New York City)

UNIT 1
I'm a little early, aren't I?

Social Language
- Make small talk
- Ask how someone would like to be addressed
- Explain customs

Vocabulary
- Ways to discuss proper address
- Manners and etiquette

Grammar
- Tag questions
- The past perfect

Preview These exercises will help prepare you for the language in the video.

A Choose the best "small talk" response for each conversation.

1. You have such a pretty name.
   a. Thank you!
   b. Please call me Dr. Smith.

2. Looks like it's going to rain today.
   a. It sure does.
   b. Is it going to rain today?

3. This office is very nice, isn't it?
   a. Thank you.
   b. As a matter of fact, it is.

4. Are you from around here?
   a. No, I'm from out of town, actually.
   b. Actually, I'm from around here.

5. I love your jacket.
   a. It's beautiful.
   b. Thank you!

B Choose the best words to complete each response.

1. **A:** Is it Mr. Rich or Dr. Rich?
   B: It's Mr., but you can just call me by my (first / last) name.

2. **A:** Is it Miss or Mrs.?
   B: Oh, I'm married. But I prefer to be called (Ms. / Miss) Park.

3. **A:** Do you mind if I call you by your first name?
   B: (Of course / Of course not). Please do.

4. **A:** Are you Ms. Novak?
   B: Yes. But there's no need to be so (formal / informal). Please call me Karen.

Beautiful day, isn't it?

Yes, it is.

Now, is it Ms. LePage or Mrs. LePage?

Um, it's Ms., but you can call me by my first name.

SCENE 1
running time — 2:40

What's taking so long?

Sneak peek

View Read each exercise and then watch the video for the answers.

A Which topics does Mrs. Beatty comment on to Marie?
- ☐ her name
- ☐ the time
- ☐ the weather
- ☑ her nationality
- ☑ her occupation
- ☐ her vacation

B Complete the scripts, according to what Mrs. Beatty says in the video.

1. "That's fine. I'm a little early, _____ I?"
2. "I'm keeping you from your work, _____ I?"
3. "I understand. You're not from here, _____ you?"
4. "That's nice. It sure is a beautiful day, _____ it?"

C Choose the best answer for each question.

1. Why is Mrs. Beatty at the office?
   a. to talk to Cheryl
   b. to talk to Mr. Evans
   c. neither of the above

2. Whom is Marie getting information for?
   a. Mrs. Beatty
   b. Mr. Evans
   c. neither of the above

3. What does Mrs. Beatty like the sound of?
   a. Marie's first name
   b. Marie's last name
   c. neither of the above

4. Why does Cheryl take Mrs. Beatty to Mr. Evans's office?
   a. so Mrs. Beatty can talk to Mr. Evans right away
   b. so Marie can finish her work
   c. so Cheryl can talk with Mrs. Beatty

Language in use

Is your last name pronounced Le-PAIGE?

It's "Le-PAHGE," **actually**.

You come from France, don't you?

Yes. Paris, **actually**.

People say **actually** to correct information or to add more information.

Extend

These exercises will help improve your fluency.

Activate your grammar

Tag questions
Use tag questions in all verb tenses to confirm information.

> I'm keeping you from your work, **aren't I?**

Statement	Tag question	Answer
You're Kazuko,	**aren't you**?	Yes, I am. / No, I'm not.
I'm on time,	**aren't I**?	Yes, you are. / No, you aren't.
You speak Thai,	**don't you**?	Yes, I do. / No, I don't.
They'll be here later,	**won't they**?	Yes, they will. / No, they won't.
They didn't know,	**did they**?	Yes, they did. / No, they didn't.
It's a beautiful day,	**isn't it**?	Yes, it is. / No, it isn't.
It isn't 1:00 yet,	**is it**?	Yes, it is. / No, it isn't.

D Complete each tag question.

1. You'll call me later, _____?
2. Your son is three years old, _____?
3. We're coming back here after dinner, _____?
4. Our teachers are pretty good, _____?
5. Your father isn't really an actor, _____?
6. My daughter didn't call when I was gone, _____?
7. You'll write when you get there, _____?
8. They should lock the door, _____?
9. Your kids wouldn't mind, _____?
10. You can use your cell phone, _____?

Expand your vocabulary

Ways to discuss proper address

Do you mind if I call you _____?
Would it be rude to call you _____?
— Not at all.
— Actually, I prefer _____.

What would you like to be called?
How do you prefer to be addressed?
— You can call me _____.
— Please call me _____.
— You can call me by my first name.

Do you use Ms. or Mrs.?
— Actually, I prefer _____.
— I use _____. Thanks for asking.

E On a separate sheet of paper, write a video script in which two people meet for the first time and engage in small talk. Ask about proper address and use tag questions.

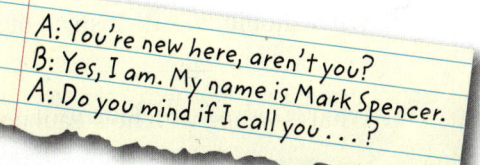

> A: You're new here, aren't you?
> B: Yes, I am. My name is Mark Spencer.
> A: Do you mind if I call you . . . ?

Speaking option: With your classmates, act out your script.

3

SCENE 2

running time — 1:17

View
Read each exercise and then watch the video for the answers.

A Check the topics Mr. Rashid and Paul discuss.
- ☑ using proper greetings
- ☐ using first and last names
- ☐ using proper titles
- ☑ pointing
- ☑ using hand gestures to say, "Come with me"
- ☐ using hand gestures to say, "Go"
- ☑ knowing how close to stand next to someone
- ☐ knowing what foods not to offer someone

Language in use

Hi, there!

People use **Hi, there!** as a friendly, informal way to say *Hello*.

B Circle the letter of the correct choice.

1. Paul pretends to be _____.
   a. an Indian tourist   b. himself

2. Mr. Rashid pretends to be _____.
   a. an Indian tourist   b. himself

3. According to Mr. Rashid, Indian women generally _____.
   a. shake hands with men
   b. do not shake hands with men

4. Paul _____.
   a. learns how to properly shake hands with an Indian tourist
   b. learns how to properly greet an Indian tourist

5. What does Paul do correctly?
   a. point
   b. bow

C Answer each question in your own words.

1. What is wrong when Paul tries to shake hands?
   _____

2. What does Paul do wrong when he waves his hand and says, "Hi, there!"?
   _____

3. What does Paul do wrong when he says, "I'm sorry"?
   _____

4. What should Paul do instead of shaking hands?
   _____

5. What is wrong with how Paul points at the bus?
   _____

4   UNIT 1

D Complete the scripts, according to what Mr. Rashid says in the video.

1. "If I were an Indian woman, you would have just insulted me. _____ generally _____."

2. "You just told me _____ _____."

3. "Oh, _____. You should stand _____ from someone."

4. "This is a rude gesture in India. _____."

5. "_____ is considered impolite. _____ instead."

Extend
These exercises will help improve your fluency.

Expand your vocabulary

Manners and etiquette

etiquette: the rules of polite behavior

table manners: polite behavior when eating with other people

punctuality: being on time

forms of address: ways of calling someone by name

gestures: how one uses one's body to communicate

impolite: not polite, rude

offensive: extremely rude or impolite

customary: usual or traditional in a particular culture

taboo: not allowed because of very strong cultural or religious rules

E Write some rules for behavior in your country. Use the manners and etiquette vocabulary.

Table manners
It's considered offensive to eat with your fingers at the table.

Table manners

Punctuality

Forms of address

Gestures

Language you know
It's OK to …
It wouldn't be offensive to …
It's considered polite to …
It might be rude to …
It wouldn't be a good idea to …
It's considered offensive to …

Speaking option: Compare your rules with a classmate's.

F On a separate sheet of paper, write a video script in which someone explains the rules of etiquette to a visitor to your country.

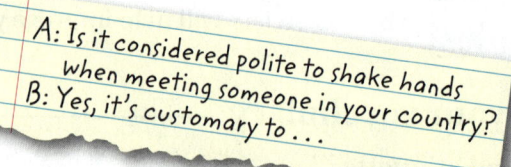

A: Is it considered polite to shake hands when meeting someone in your country?
B: Yes, it's customary to …

Speaking option: Act out your script with a classmate.

Activate your grammar

The past perfect

                had   +   past participle
By 2001, she **had** already **met** her husband.

Use the past perfect to describe something that happened before a specific time in the past.
    By April, he **had started** his new job.
    At 3:00, we **hadn't** yet **heard** the news.

Use the past perfect with the simple past tense to show which of two past events occurred first.
    I **had** already **seen** the movie when it came out on DVD. (First I saw it. Then it came out on DVD.)

Note: In informal speech, people often use the simple past tense instead of the past perfect. The words *before* and *after* can help clarify the order of events in informal speech.
    By April, he **started** his new job.
    Before I graduated, I **learned** to speak Greek.
    I became a good driver after I **got** my own car.

G Complete each sentence with the words in parentheses. Use the past perfect.

1. When Paul arrived, Mr. Evans (already / decide) _____ to have Mr. Rashid teach him about etiquette.

2. Paul shook Mr. Rashid's hand because Mr. Rashid (ask) _____ him to greet him as if he were an Indian tourist.

3. Mr. Rashid corrected Paul right away because he (already / use) _____ an insulting gesture.

4. Even before Mr. Rashid corrected his gesture for "over there," Paul already knew that he probably (insult) _____ someone.

5. Paul felt bad, but Mr. Rashid assured him he (do) _____ a good job.

6. Finally, Paul laughed, because he (make) _____ so many mistakes.

H On a separate sheet of paper, summarize the video episode, using the past perfect to clarify the order of events.

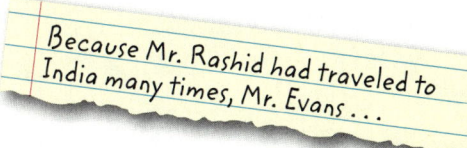

Because Mr. Rashid had traveled to India many times, Mr. Evans...

TOP NOTCH POP SONG   It's a Great Day for Love
running time — 3:34

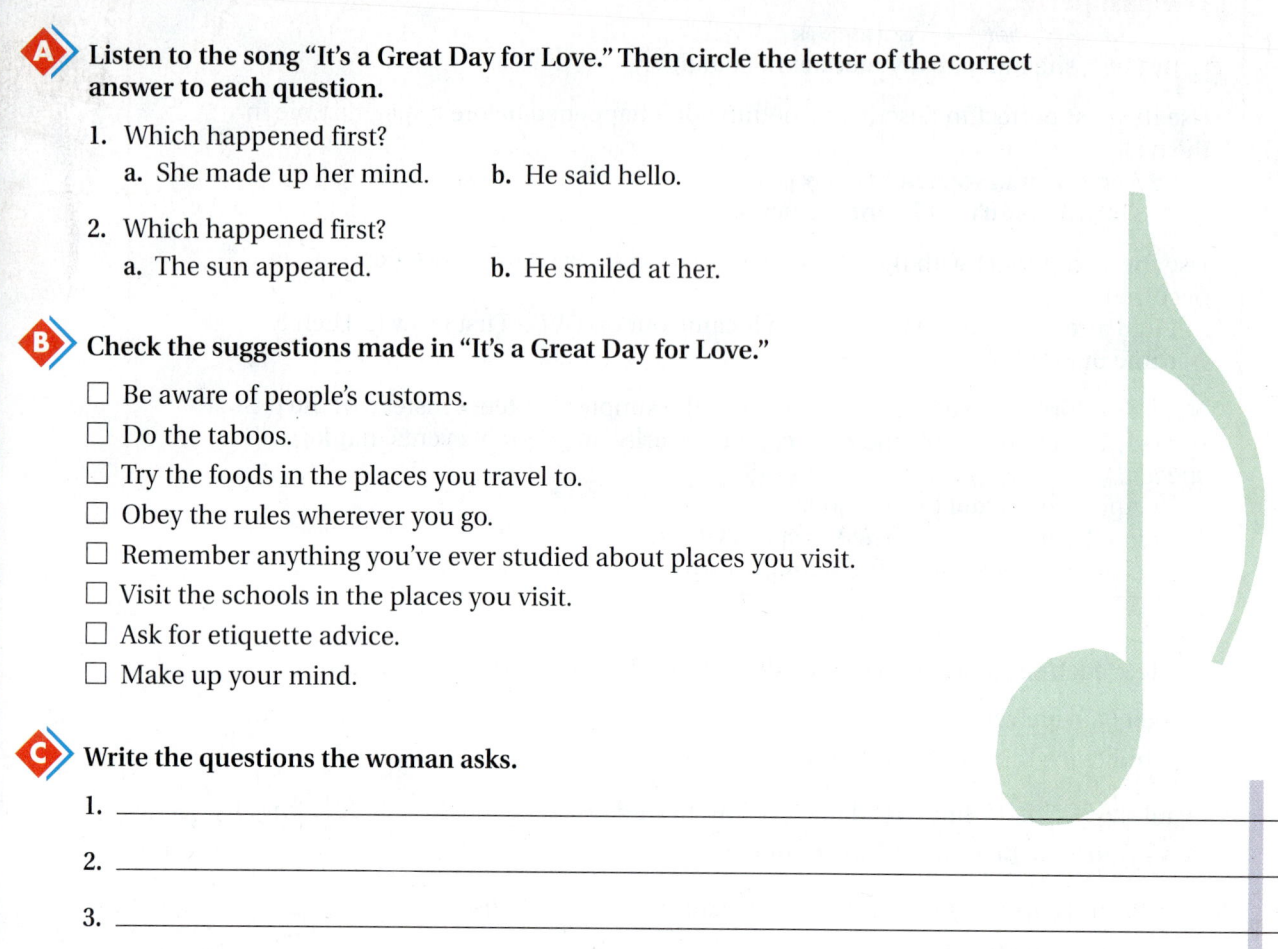

A Listen to the song "It's a Great Day for Love." Then circle the letter of the correct answer to each question.

1. Which happened first?
   a. She made up her mind.
   b. He said hello.

2. Which happened first?
   a. The sun appeared.
   b. He smiled at her.

B Check the suggestions made in "It's a Great Day for Love."

☐ Be aware of people's customs.
☐ Do the taboos.
☐ Try the foods in the places you travel to.
☐ Obey the rules wherever you go.
☐ Remember anything you've ever studied about places you visit.
☐ Visit the schools in the places you visit.
☐ Ask for etiquette advice.
☐ Make up your mind.

C Write the questions the woman asks.

1. _____
2. _____
3. _____
4. _____

8   UNIT 1

UNIT 2
Are you OK?

Social Language
- Describe symptoms
- Show concern

Vocabulary
- Medical treatments and medications
- Symptoms

Grammar
- May, might, must
- Be able to

Preview These exercises will help prepare you for the language in the video.

Expand your vocabulary

Medical treatments

conventional medicine: treats illness and injury, based on Western scientific study
chiropractic: treats pain and injury, based on adjustments of bones in the spine
spiritual healing: treats illness, using the mind and/or religious faith
acupuncture: treats pain and illness by means of needles inserted at specific places in the body
herbal therapy: treats illness, using a variety of plants
homeopathic medicine: treats injury and illness, using remedies made from natural sources that are designed to help the body heal itself

Expand your vocabulary

Medications

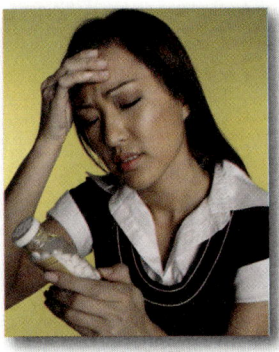

- a painkiller
- cold tablets 
- eye drops 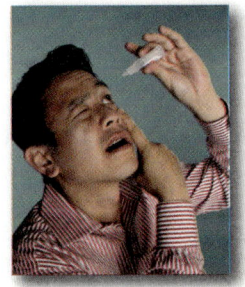
- a nasal spray / a decongestant 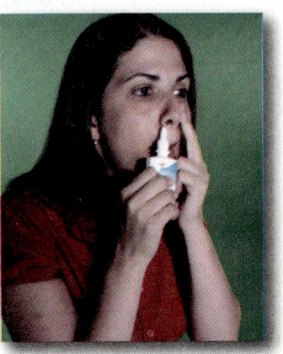
- an antihistamine  
- cough medicine 
- an antibiotic 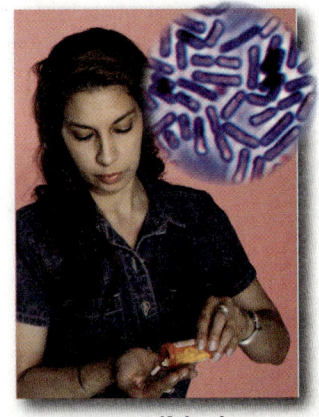
- an antacid 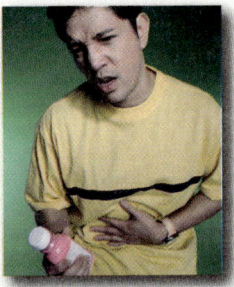
- an ointment 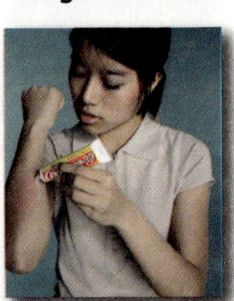
- vitamins 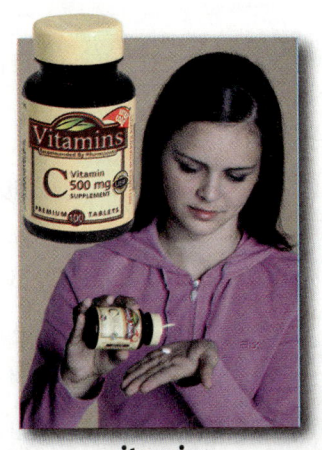

9

A Mark each statement *T* (true) or *F* (false).

___ 1. Acupuncture treats colds with antibiotics.

___ 2. Decongestants are an example of spiritual healing.

___ 3. Spiritual healing is a form of conventional medicine.

___ 4. Chiropractic is one way of treating back pain.

___ 5. Conventional medicine is based on science, not on traditional religious faith.

___ 6. Chiropractic uses nasal sprays and cold tablets.

___ 7. Homeopathic doctors manipulate the spine to treat pain.

___ 8. Herbal therapy is an effective application of religious faith.

Activate your grammar

May / might and *must*

May or *might* for possibility
Use *may* or *might* and the base form of a verb to express possibility. *May* and *might* have the same meaning.
  Acupuncture **might** [or **may**] **be** helpful for your headaches.

Must for conclusions
Use *must* and the base form of a verb when something is almost certainly true.
  You have a terrible cold. It **must be** really hard to breathe.
  She came to work today. She **must not have** a cold anymore.

Be able to for ability
Be able to has the same meaning as *can*. It can follow *may*, *might*, or *must* and often has future meaning.
  I **might not be able to get** there on time for my 3:00 appointment tomorrow.
  She took the medicine, so she**'ll be able to work** tomorrow.

B Answer each question. Use *may* or *might* and, where appropriate, *be able to*.

1. What kind of treatment do you think you will use the next time you have a cold? _____

2. What remedies will you recommend to other people? _____

3. Do you think you can work tomorrow? _____

C Complete each conclusion with *must* or *must not*.

1. **Evan:** I heard you had a bad backache. I'm so sorry. That _____ make it hard to work.
   Dan: Thanks, Evan. It really does hurt a lot.

2. **Sara:** Allen's not here yet. He _____ be at the pharmacy.
   Steve: No, he just called. He's stuck in traffic.

3. **Cassie:** Peter's still coughing. That medicine _____ be working.
   Martin: I think you're right.

SCENE 1
running time — 2:01

Sneak peek

"I feel awful."

View — Read each exercise and then watch the video for the answers.

A Complete the video scripts. Use the verb phrases with *may*, *might*, and *must* that you hear.

1. Let's get Ms. Novak's tickets ready. She _____ this afternoon.

2. You _____ see a doctor.

3. Paul, you really _____ some medical help.

4. A little acupuncture _____ you feel better.

5. Dr. Anderson is meeting Mr. Evans downstairs in the café. Should we ask her to come up? She _____.

6. You _____ an herbal remedy.

11

B Choose the best answer for each question.

1. What's the problem with Paul?
   a. He feels awful.
   b. He's allergic to doctors.
   c. He doesn't want to see Ms. Novak.

2. Which two physical symptoms does he complain of?
   a. a headache and a stomachache
   b. hip and back pain
   c. nausea and sneezing

3. Who suggests he see a doctor?
   a. Marie and Cheryl
   b. Cheryl and Bob
   c. Bob and Marie

4. Who used to want to be a doctor?
   a. Marie
   b. Paul
   c. Bob

5. What treatments does Bob suggest?
   a. acupuncture, herbal medicine, and spiritual healing
   b. conventional medicine and chiropractic
   c. antibiotics, decongestants, and herbal medicine

6. What makes Paul feel worse?
   a. medicine
   b. treatment
   c. laughter

Language in use

Want to try a little spiritual healing?

In informal spoken English, it's common to drop *Do you* and begin questions directly with the base form. (*Do you* want to . . .)

C Mark each statement *T* (true) or *F* (false).

___ 1. Paul is pretending to be sick so he won't have to work.
___ 2. Bob wants to be a doctor.
___ 3. Paul has been sick since last night.
___ 4. Paul wants to laugh.
___ 5. Marie is going to call and make a doctor's appointment for Paul.
___ 6. Paul dislikes going to the doctor.

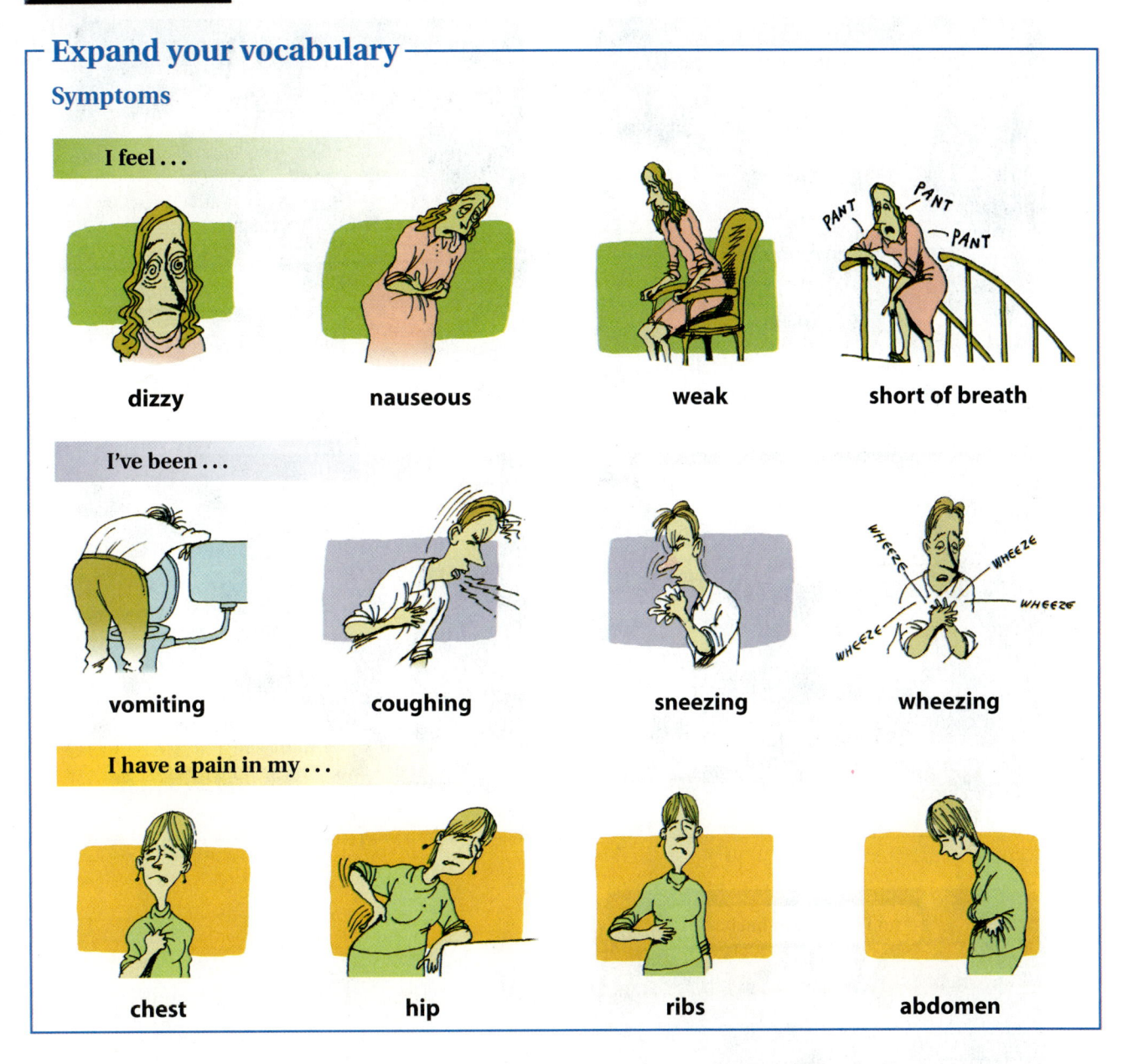

Extend These exercises will help improve your fluency.

Expand your vocabulary

Symptoms

I feel . . .

dizzy | nauseous | weak | short of breath

I've been . . .

vomiting | coughing | sneezing | wheezing

I have a pain in my . . .

chest | hip | ribs | abdomen

D List three symptoms, illnesses, or physical problems you have or have had. What remedy or treatment did you use? Did it help?

Ailment	Remedy or treatment	Did it help?

Speaking option: Compare your ailments and remedies with those of a classmate.

E Write your own suggestion to Paul for each of his problems. Use *may* or *might*.

1. *A decongestant might help your cold.*

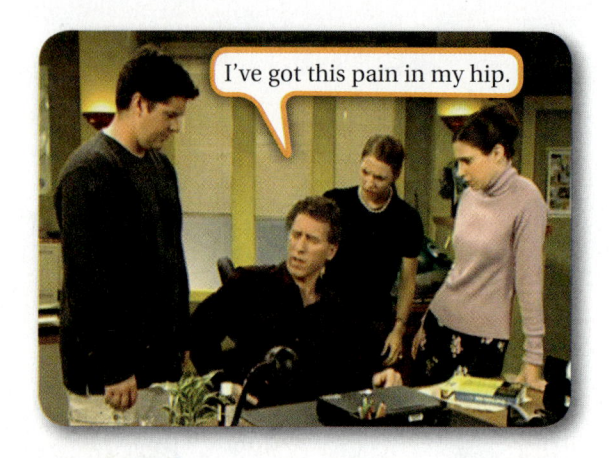

2. _____

3. _____

4. _____

5. _____

SCENE 2

running time — 1:39

> Have you taken any medications lately?

Sneak peek

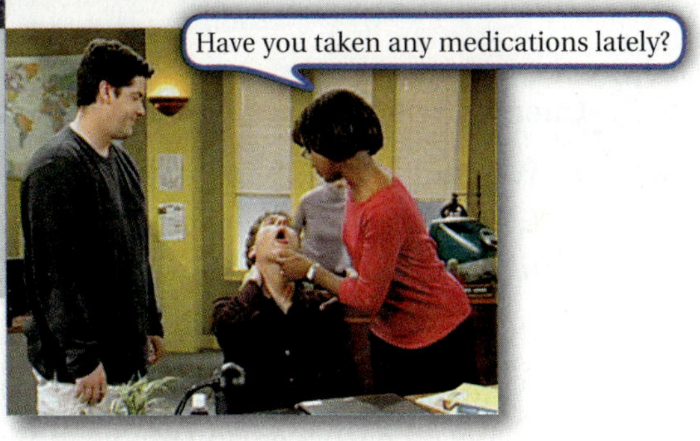

View Read each exercise and then watch the video for the answers.

A Check the remedies and medications that are mentioned in the video episode.

- ☐ painkillers
- ☐ eye drops
- ☐ cold tablets
- ☐ nasal spray
- ☐ antibiotics
- ☐ cough medicines
- ☐ vitamins
- ☐ antacids
- ☐ decongestants

B Write the name of the person who made each of the following statements or asked the following questions.

Paul    Marie    Bob    Dr. Anderson    Cheryl

_____ 1. "That's a lot of medicine."

_____ 2. "Stay away from me!"

_____ 3. "What about the other stuff? The pain in the back and the side . . . ?"

_____ 4. "Well, that explains it. You exercised too much."

_____ 5. "Just some over-the-counter stuff—painkiller, cold tablets, nasal spray."

_____ 6. "A little chiropractic treatment might help you."

_____ 7. "That must be why you're feeling so bad."

15

C Choose the best answer for each question.

1. Why does Bob tell Dr. Anderson to cover her face?
   a. so she won't catch Paul's cold
   b. so she won't sneeze
   c. so she won't give Paul a cold

2. What does Dr. Anderson want to know?
   a. if Paul has taken any medications lately
   b. if Paul has a cold
   c. if Bob has back pain, too

3. What does Dr. Anderson say about the medications Paul has taken?
   a. that they weren't effective
   b. that there were too many of them
   c. that they might help

4. Who is Don?
   a. the friend Paul exercised with
   b. the acupuncturist Paul went to see
   c. the friend Paul gave his cold to

5. When did Paul start his new exercise routine?
   a. the week before
   b. the night before
   c. Paul doesn't exercise.

6. What does Dr. Anderson think caused Paul's problem?
   a. too little medicine
   b. too much chiropractic
   c. too much exercise

Language in use

Cover your face, **Doc**.

Doc (very informal) = doctor. It should not be used unless one knows the doctor very well or is a friend.

Extend
These exercises will help improve your fluency.

D Summarize what happens in the video episode.

Paul is sick . . .

_____

_____

_____

_____

_____

E On a separate sheet of paper, write a short video script of a conversation between a doctor and a patient. Include suggestions for treatments and medications.

A: My throat is killing me.
B: Have you taken any medications?
A: Just . . .

Speaking option: Act out your video script with a classmate.

16   UNIT 2

ON-THE-STREET INTERVIEWS

Are you traditional in your medical ideas?

running time — 1:38

View

Read each exercise and then watch the video for the answers.

Joe   James   Vanessa   Lisa

A Choose the best answer for each question.

1. Who would rather use herbal and natural remedies than conventional medicine?
   a. Vanessa   **b.** James   **c.** Joe

2. Who hasn't explored nontraditional medicine but thinks it may have many advantages?
   a. Vanessa   **b.** Lisa   **c.** Joe

3. Which interviewee suggests that traditional medicine might be dangerous?
   a. Vanessa   **b.** Joe   **c.** James

4. Which interviewees mention nontraditional therapies they use or have used?
   a. James and Joe   **b.** Vanessa and Lisa   **c.** James and Vanessa

5. Which interviewee doesn't say anything good about nontraditional medicine?
   a. Vanessa   **b.** Lisa   **c.** James

B Complete the interviewer's questions from the video.

1. "Are you traditional in your medical ideas? That is, do you kind of _____, or do you like to explore _____, such as _____?"

2. "In your opinion, _____ of traditional Western _____?"

3. "What do you see as maybe some _____?"

4. "Are there any _____?"

17

Extend These exercises will help improve your fluency.

C Answer the questions.

1. Are you traditional in your medical ideas? Explain.
   _____
   _____

2. What do you think are the advantages of traditional Western medicine?
   _____
   _____

3. How about some of the disadvantages?
   _____
   _____

4. What are some non-traditional therapies you've used?
   _____
   _____

Speaking option: Use the questions to interview a classmate. Tell the class about his or her views.

D On a separate sheet of paper, write a paragraph about your beliefs about medicine and therapies. Use the interview questions from Exercise B and your answers from Exercise C as a guide.

Medical treatments and medications
conventional (or traditional) medicine
nontraditional medicine
Western medicine
acupuncture
homeopathic medicine
spiritual healing
herbal medicine
chiropractic
vitamins

18 UNIT 2

UNIT 3
I need to get a package to Australia a.s.a.p.!

Social Language
- Request express service
- Recommend a service provider
- Plan a social event

Vocabulary
- Services
- Service providers
- Adjectives to describe services

Grammar
- The passive causative
- Causatives *get*, *have*, and *make*
- *Let*

Preview These exercises will help prepare you for the language in the video.

Activate your grammar

The passive causative

Use *get* or *have* with an object and the past participle to talk about arranging services. *Get* and *have* have the same meaning in the passive causative.

	get / have	**object**	**past participle**	
They	had	the package	delivered	by Air Express.
We need to	get	this document	printed	as soon as possible.
I	'm having	the office	cleaned	tomorrow.
He can	get	his car	repaired	this afternoon.

A *by* phrase is used when the speaker thinks that information is important.
We're having the office cleaned **by Royal Cleaning Services**.
They got the copier repaired yesterday. (not necessary to know by whom)

Hello. I need to **get** twenty-five color documents **printed** right away.

A Complete the phone requests for express service, using the passive causative with *have* or *get*.

1. Hello, Perfection Dry Cleaners? Would it be possible to _____ by 3:00 P.M.?
   my suit / clean
2. Bart's Auto Body? Hi. I want to _____ right away. Can you fit me in?
   my car / repaint
3. Is this Speedy Copy Services? This is a rush job. Can I _____ this morning?
   200 color documents / copy
4. Hello, Air Express? I'd like to _____ to Europe by tomorrow. Can I do that?
   a package / send
5. Hello, Top Notch Travel? Would it be possible to _____ today?
   our plane tickets / deliver

19

Activate your grammar

Causative *have*

Use the causative *have* to show that one person causes another person to do something. Use a form of *have* + an object and a base form of a verb.

		object	base form	
She	**had**	her assistant	**plan**	the meeting.
I'll	**have**	the receptionist	**call**	you tomorrow.

> I called ten restaurants and **had** them **give** us a price for a party room.

B Use the cues and the verbs in the box to write sentences using the causative *have*. Use each verb only once.

explain   make   meet   pick up   prepare

1. Why don't you / your assistant / a reservation at the restaurant?
   _____

2. I'm going to / the tour guide / how to get there.
   _____

3. She / her husband / the package at the airport last week.
   _____

4. At our wedding last year, we / the chef / a special dish for our guests.
   _____

5. You can / the tour bus / the group in front of the bus station.
   _____

C Cross out and correct the mistake in each sentence.

1. Can you have your assistant ~~delivered~~ *deliver* the package tomorrow?
2. Where did you have made those color prints?
3. I get my house to clean by a cleaning service.
4. We had our car repair last week.
5. I'll have make my secretary some coffee for you.
6. Our office manager got the copier to repair yesterday.
7. Did you have your assistant called the manager?

SCENE 1

running time — 2:00

Sneak peek

Mr. Wells needs those documents the day after tomorrow!

View Read each exercise and then watch the video for the answers.

A Complete each statement with the correct name.

Paul   Cheryl   Bob   Marie   Mr. Evans

1. _____ is going to have the courier pick up the package.
2. _____ is going to reprint the tour information.
3. _____ is going to have the travel guides printed.
4. _____ is going to reprint the tickets.
5. _____ is going to have his sleeves shortened.

B Circle the correct word or name to complete each statement.

1. (Cheryl / Mr. Evans) gave the travel documents to (Mr. Wells / Mr. Rashid).
2. (Mr. Rashid / Mr. Wells) needs the travel documents (the day after tomorrow / by 5:00).
3. Marie has (National Express / Copies To Go) deliver the travel documents to (Australia / Lebanon).
4. (Cheryl / Paul) calls (Copies To Go / Harper's) to request a rush job.
5. (Bob / Mr. Evans) calls (a courier / a tailor) to request a rush job.

Language in use

A white envelope **about this big**?

People gesture and say **about this big / long / high** to indicate the size, length, or height of something.

21

C Complete the scripts, according to what they say in the video.

1. Now, about the travel documents for the Australian group. We've _____, right?

2. Mr. Evans, _____ of travel documents _____ the other night at dinner, before he flew home to Sydney.

3. I'll call Copies To Go and _____ _____ the travel guides.

4. Hello. I need to _____ _____ right away.

Extend
These exercises will help improve your fluency.

Expand your vocabulary

Some services

- dry-clean a suit
- frame a picture 
- lengthen / shorten a skirt 
- enlarge photos 

D On a separate sheet of paper, write about the services you've had performed recently. Use the passive causative. Were you pleased with the services?

I had two sweaters dry-cleaned last week at Larry's Cleaners. They did a great job!

Speaking option: Tell a classmate about the services you listed.

Extend

These exercises will help improve your fluency.

Expand your vocabulary

Some service providers

- a copy service
- a housecleaning service 
- a car repair shop 
- a courier service 
- a dry cleaner 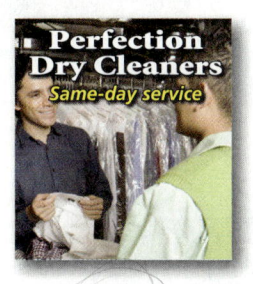
- a tailor 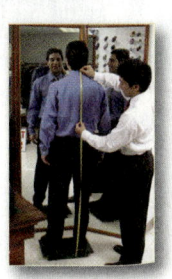
- a catering service 

Adjectives to describe services
reliable: can be trusted to keep a promise
reasonable: doesn't charge too much money
fast: does the job in a short time
honest: does not lie or cheat
efficient: doesn't waste time
helpful: is willing to help
professional: does a very good job

E List the service providers you use regularly. Describe what you think of their service.

Service provider	Type of service	Description
Modern Auto	car repair shop	They're reliable, reasonable, and very professional.

Service provider	Type of service	Description

Speaking option: Tell the class about the service providers you use regularly. Does anyone use the same service providers? Compare your opinions of the providers.

SCENE 2
running time — 1:34

Sneak peek: Bob, I'll let you choose the menu. You will?

View — Read each exercise and then watch the video for the answers.

A Match the people with what they are thinking.

___ 1. Mr. Evans ___ 2. Cheryl ___ 3. Bob ___ 4. Marie ___ 5. Paul

a. I'd like all of you to plan the party.
b. I'd like to choose where we have the party.
c. I'd like to choose what to have for the entrée.
d. I'd like to choose the entertainment.
e. I'd like to do everything.

B Mark each statement *T* (true), *F* (false), or *NI* (no information).

___ 1. The staff is planning a party for Mr. Wells's family.
___ 2. The party will be the next day.
___ 3. Cheryl wants Marie to call ten different restaurants for prices.
___ 4. Marie would be happy to choose the restaurant.
___ 5. Bob eats steak and potatoes every day.
___ 6. Mr. Wells would prefer chicken or fish for the menu.
___ 7. Paul would prefer to have rock music at the party.
___ 8. Marie and Paul have a lot to do to help plan the party.

Language in use

I like chicken more than fish, **I guess**.

People say **I guess** when they are not sure or don't really have a strong opinion about something.

C Complete each of Cheryl's statements from the video with the causative *have*.

1. "Marie, I'd like to _____ a restaurant for the party."

2. "Now, Marie, I called ten restaurants and _____ us a price for a party room. These two had the best prices."

3. "Well, the client asked for fish or chicken. So I _____ together a menu with each. Which do you like better?"

24 UNIT 3

Extend These exercises will help improve your fluency.

Activate your grammar

Causatives *get* and *make*

The causative *get* has the same meaning as the causative *have*. With *get*, use an object and an infinitive.

	object	infinitive	
I **got**	my brother	**to help**	me finish the job.

Use the causative *make* to suggest an obligation. With *make*, use an object and a base form.

	object	base form	
I **made**	my brother	**help**	me finish the job.

Let

Use *let* with an object and a base form of a verb to show that one person permits another person to do something.

	object	base form	
She **let**	her sister	**wear**	her skirt.

D Circle the correct word to complete each sentence.

1. Cheryl decides she's going to (make / let) Paul choose the music.
2. Mr. Evans (gets / lets) Cheryl to plan the party.
3. Cheryl (gets / makes) Marie choose between two restaurants.
4. Paul (lets / makes) Cheryl choose her own music.
5. Cheryl (gets / lets) Bob to choose chicken for the entrée.
6. Cheryl (gets / makes) everyone agree with her choices.

E On a separate sheet of paper, write a story about what happened at the meeting. Use *let* and the causatives *get*, *have*, and *make*.

> Mr. Evans wanted to have a party for one of the tour groups, so he got Cheryl to plan it...

Speaking option: Tell your story to a classmate.

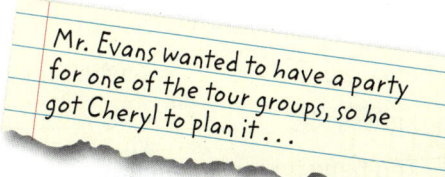

F Write a list of steps you would take if you were going to plan a party in a restaurant. Use *let* and the causatives *get*, *have*, and *make* and the passive causative.

> First, I would get someone to help me choose a restaurant...

Sequence words
First,...   After that,...
Then,...   Finally,...

Speaking option: With a partner, plan a party for some "important guests." Then tell the class about your plans.

25

TOP NOTCH POP SONG   I'll Get Back to You

running time — 2:52

A Listen to the song "I'll Get Back to You." Then listen without looking at the screen and complete the lyrics.

Your camera isn't working right.
It needs a few repairs.
You _____ overnight.
       1.
Nothing else compares.
You had to _____,
            2.
and now you want to _____
                     3.
someone to _____ your fancy shirts
           4.
and _____ when they're wet.
    5.
Come a little closer—
let me whisper in your ear.
Is my message getting across
to you loud and clear?

You're always making plans.
I'll tell you what I'll do:
let me think it over and
I'll get back to you.

You want to _____.
             6.
You want to _____ someone
            7.
to _____ your new pair of jeans
   8.
and _____ you when they're done.
    9.
I guess I'll _____ a sign
             10.
and hang it on your shelf,
with four small words in one big line:

"Just do it yourself."
Let me tell you what this song
is really all about.
I'm getting tired of waiting while you
figure it out.
I've heard all your demands,
but I have a life, too.
Let me think it over and
I'll get back to you.

I'm really reliable,
incredibly fast,
extremely helpful
from first to last.
Let me see what I can do.
Day after day,
everybody knows
I always do what I say.

You're always making plans.
I'll tell you what I'll do:
let me think it over and
I'll get back to you.

B On a separate sheet of paper, answer the questions about the song. Use the passive causative.

1. What did she want done with her new skirt?
2. What does she want done with her fancy shirts?
3. What things does he want done?
4. What message does she want hung on his shelf?

26   UNIT 3

UNIT 4
I could have been a great dancer.

Social Language
- Explain life choices
- Express regrets

Vocabulary
- Skills and abilities

Grammar
- The future in the past
- Perfect modals

Preview These exercises will help prepare you for the language in the video.

Activate your grammar

Future in the past: *was / were going to* and *would*

was / were going to + base form
Use for future plans one had in the past.
> She **was going to buy** a car last week, but she changed her mind.
> We thought we **were going to see** that movie, but they showed something else.

would + base form
Use for future plans one had in the past, but only after statements of knowledge or belief.
> I thought I **would be** a teacher, but I decided to do something else.
> They always knew they **would get** married, and they did.
> She thought she **would buy** a car last week, but she changed her mind.

A Complete the statements about the plans for the future each character had. Use the future in the past.

> I'm going to get married at age 18.

Cheryl, age 10

> I don't think I'm going to get married.

Marie, age 9

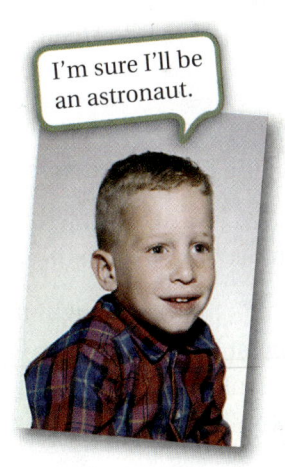

> I'm sure I'll be an astronaut.

Paul, age 5

1. When she was young, Cheryl thought _____.

2. When she was young, Marie believed _____.

3. When he was young, Paul was sure _____.

27

SCENE 1
running time — 2:36

I really enjoy cooking, actually.

Sneak peek

View Read each exercise and then watch the video for the answers.

A Complete each of Cheryl's statements from the video.

1. "When I was young, I thought I _____ a chef."

2. "My mother talked me out of it. She _____ always _____ at night. She _____ I _____ never _____ a man and get married."

3. "Hey, you'll never guess what Bob _____."

4. "Bob _____ a dancer."

Activate your grammar

Perfect modals

To express regrets about past actions, use *should have* + a past participle.
   I **shouldn't have studied** French; I **should have studied** Russian instead.

To speculate about the past, use *would have, could have, may / might have* + a past participle.
   They **may have made** a mistake, but it **could have been** worse.

To draw conclusions about the past, use *must have* + a past participle.
   I'm surprised she decided to be a teacher. She **must have known** that teachers don't earn a lot of money.

B Choose the phrase that best completes each statement about the video episode.

1. Cheryl _____ a chef.
   a. must have been   b. couldn't have been   c. could have been

2. Cheryl's mother thought that Cheryl _____ a chef.
   a. must have been crazy to want to be
   b. shouldn't have been
   c. wouldn't have been happy if she had been

3. Paul agreed that if Cheryl had been a chef she _____ Bob.
   a. wouldn't have met
   b. must not have met
   c. shouldn't have met

4. Bob thinks that he _____ a great dancer.
   a. must have been
   b. could have been
   c. shouldn't have been

5. If the diet hadn't been so difficult, Bob _____ to be a dancer.
   a. must have been able
   b. couldn't have been able
   c. might have been able

Language in use

Hey, you'll never guess what Bob was going to be.

People say **Hey, you'll never guess**... to introduce surprising information.

28 UNIT 4

Extend

These exercises will help improve your fluency.

C Answer the questions with complete sentences

1. What did Cheryl think she was going to be when she was younger?
   _____

2. Why did she change her mind?
   _____

3. What did Cheryl's mother think would happen if Cheryl didn't choose another career?
   _____

4. Why does Paul think Cheryl wouldn't have met Bob if she had become a chef?
   _____

5. Why didn't Bob become a dancer?
   _____

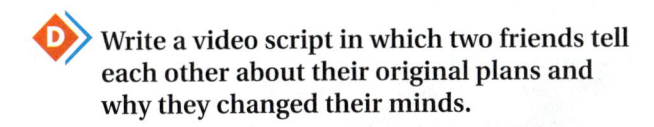

D Write a video script in which two friends tell each other about their original plans and why they changed their minds.

> A: When I was young, I thought I would be a doctor.
> B: Well, why did you change your mind?
> A: I got interested in history instead. But sometimes I think I should have studied medicine . . .

Speaking option: Act out your video script with a classmate.

E Write three plans or thoughts you had about your future when you were young. Then write what you actually did. Finally, write a statement with a perfect modal, speculating, drawing a conclusion, or expressing regret.

> 1. When I was young, I thought I would grow up and live in a big city. However, I decided I liked life in a smaller town. I actually think I would have been unhappy in a big city.

1. _____
   _____

2. _____
   _____

3. _____
   _____

Speaking option: Tell your classmates about your plans, regrets, conclusions, and/or speculations.

SCENE 2
running time — 2:00

Sneak peek: I think I would have made a great television etiquette teacher.

View — Read each exercise and then watch the video for the answers.

A Check the reasons mentioned in the video for why Mr. Evans would have been a good etiquette instructor on TV.

- ☐ He's very polite.
- ☐ He wrote a book about etiquette.
- ☐ He studied etiquette in school.
- ☐ He knows which fork to use.
- ☐ He knows the customs of other cultures.
- ☐ He tries not to laugh.

B Complete the scripts, according to what they say in the video.

1. What about you, Mr. Evans? _____ when you were younger?

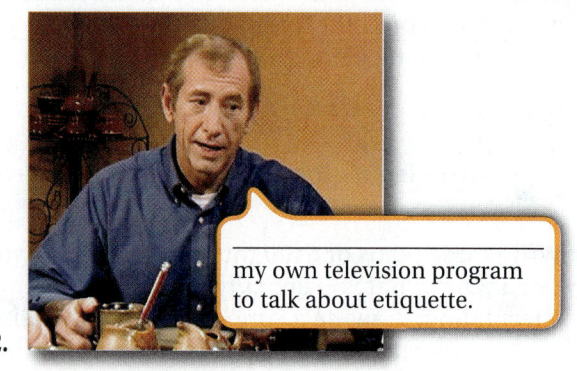

2. _____ my own television program to talk about etiquette.

3. I have always loved etiquette. I think I _____ a great television etiquette teacher.

4. You've taught me a lot _____.

30   UNIT 4

C Complete each statement with the name of the correct character from the video episode.

1. _____ wants to know what life plans Mr. Evans had when he was younger.
2. _____ thinks it's not too late for Mr. Evans to become a television etiquette teacher.
3. _____ says Mr. Evans has taught him a lot.
4. _____ says Mr. Evans always knows which fork to use in a restaurant.
5. _____ is surprised to learn that Mr. Evans is so interested in etiquette.

D Read each false statement. Cross out and correct the false information to make the statement true.

1. ~~Bob~~ *Mr. Evans* thought he'd teach etiquette on television one day.
2. Paul gives a speech about the reasons international guests may look offended when they have dinner with you.
3. The name of Mr. Evans's imaginary television etiquette program is *International Customs with Evans*.
4. Mr. Evans hopes the others will be amused when they hear what his plans once were.
5. Mr. Evans has recently become interested in etiquette.

Language in use

The positive exclamations **Wow**, **Amazing**, and **Unforgettable** can be said with flat intonation to express sarcasm—to suggest the opposite of their original meaning.

Extend These exercises will help improve your fluency.

Expand your vocabulary

Skills and abilities

talents: abilities in art, music, languages, etc., that you are born with.
I was lucky to be born with talent in languages. I learn them easily and quickly.

skills: abilities that you learn, such as speaking a particular foreign language or playing a particular musical instrument
The new travel agent at Top Notch Travel has the skills necessary for dealing with groups from many cultural backgrounds.

experience: time spent working at a job or at learning a skill
They have three years' experience in television production.

knowledge: understanding of, or familiarity with, a subject—gained from experience or study
Diana has extensive knowledge of geography. She can tell you the location of any country in the world.

E Answer the questions.

1. Bob says that Mr. Evans has a talent because he knows which fork to use. Do you think that's really a talent? If not, what do you think it is—knowledge, skill, etc.? Explain your answer.
   _____
   _____

2. What talents, experience, and skills do you have? Explain your answer and provide examples.
   _____
   _____
   _____

F Marie and Paul don't discuss what they thought they would be when they were young. On a separate sheet of paper, write a video script for a conversation between Marie and Paul about their own plans in the past. Use *was going to, would,* and perfect modals. Use the skills and abilities vocabulary.

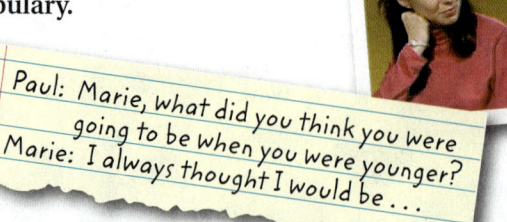

> Paul: Marie, what did you think you were going to be when you were younger?
> Marie: I always thought I would be . . .

Speaking option: Act out your video script with a classmate.

ON-THE-STREET INTERVIEWS

running time — 1:45

How would you describe your skills and abilities?

View

Read each exercise and then watch the video for the answers.

Rita   Matt   San

A Mark each statement *T* (true) or *F* (false). Cross out and correct the false information to make the false statements true.

___ 1. Rita is a university teacher.

___ 2. San is a television producer.

___ 3. Matt works in marketing.

___ 4. San isn't good at art.

___ 5. One of Matt's skills is coming up with good ideas.

B Complete each statement about the interviewees' skills and abilities.

1. Matt says one of his talents is ____.
   a. thinking up creative ideas to promote products
   b. driving fire trucks
   c. political leadership

2. Rita loves teaching children because she can share her ____ with children.
   a. abilities
   b. skills
   c. knowledge

3. San would like to use her ____ in television production and direction.
   a. mathematical skills
   b. artistic talent
   c. product knowledge

4. San believes that talents and abilities are the result of ____.
   a. genetic factors
   b. environmental factors
   c. a mix of genetic and environmental factors

Language in use

Good question.

People begin answers with **Good question** to "buy time" to think of an answer.

33

C Complete the scripts, according to what they say in the video.

1. Interviewer: Could you tell me _____?
   Rita: I'm an elementary _____.
   Matt: My _____ path _____ in marketing.
   San: _____, and _____ eventually produce and direct.

2. Interviewer: Did you _____ when you were a child?
   Matt: No. _____ president of the United States or _____ fire truck.

3. Interviewer: What made teaching _____?
   Rita: First of all, _____, and I liked _____ imparting some of my _____ to young ones.

4. Interviewer: _____ are some of your skills?
   San: I would say _____.
   Matt: My _____ would be coming up with new ideas . . .

5. Interviewer: Do you think that _____ are genetic?
   San: I think _____ of both genetics and environment.

Extend
These exercises will help improve your fluency.

D Choose one of the careers. On a separate sheet of paper, write four or five interview questions to ask a person applying for a job in that career. Use the grammar and vocabulary from this unit.

Careers
- travel agent or tour guide
- art teacher for a children's summer camp
- sales or marketing representative
- manager in a large company

Speaking option: Using your interview questions, role-play a job interview with a classmate.

E In the video, the interviewer asks if talents and abilities are genetic. What do you think? Provide details to support your answer.

_____
_____
_____
_____
_____
_____

UNIT 5
I want a large wedding.

Social Language
- Discuss a wedding
- Discuss holiday traditions

Vocabulary
- Getting married
- Ways to describe a holiday
- Ways to commemorate a holiday

Grammar
- Adjective clauses with subject relative pronouns
- Adjective clauses with object relative pronouns

Preview
These exercises will help prepare you for the language in the video.

Expand your vocabulary

Getting married

an engagement: an agreement to marry someone (*get engaged / be engaged*)

a wedding ceremony: a formal set of actions in which two people get married

a bride: a woman at the time she gets married

a groom: a man at the time he gets married

newlyweds: the bride and groom after the wedding

a guest: a person who is invited to a wedding

a reception: a large formal party or celebration for the bride and groom after a wedding ceremony

a honeymoon: a vacation taken by two newlyweds after their wedding (*go on* a *honeymoon*)

traditional: following customs that have existed for a long time
contemporary: modern

I prefer traditional music in the ceremony.

Contemporary music.

A Complete the letter with the vocabulary words.

Dear Kate,

I've got some great news! My daughter, Alison, is getting married! She and her boyfriend, Stan, got _____1_____ a week ago, and they're planning to get married at the end of June. Now that Alison is going to be a _____2_____, all she thinks and talks about is the wedding. She wants to invite at least two hundred _____3_____. The _____4_____ will be held outdoors in Taft Park, which is a gorgeous setting, and the _____5_____ afterward will be held at the Switwald Center, about ten minutes away.

Even though a lot of young people are choosing to have more contemporary wedding ceremonies, Alison wants a very _____6_____ ceremony. For example, she insists that Stan, since he's the _____7_____, not see her on their wedding day until the ceremony begins. She thinks that would be bad luck. I guess she's old-fashioned—just like her father!

George and I have agreed that after the wedding we are going to pay to send the _____8_____ on a spectacular _____9_____. They deserve it! I'll let you know the exact date soon. I really hope you can make it!

Regards,
Mona

35

SCENE 1

running time — 2:34

I'd like a long ceremony, and a short reception.

I want a short ceremony, and a huge celebration afterwards.

View Read each exercise and then watch the video for the answers.

A What ideas do Bob and Cheryl have about each wedding detail? Complete the chart.

	Bob	Cheryl
The number of guests		
The location of the ceremony		
The type of music at the ceremony		
The length of the ceremony		
The length of the reception		
The type of wedding cake		

B Circle the correct choice to complete each sentence.

1. Bob thinks planning a wedding is _____.
   a. fun   b. difficult   c. interesting

2. Marie is _____.
   a. happy to help   b. too busy to help   c. not sure she wants to help

3. Cheryl wants to invite lots of _____.
   a. friends   b. co-workers   c. family members

4. Marie thinks an outdoor wedding might be _____.
   a. very nice   b. uncomfortable   c. expensive

5. Cheryl thinks Marie's ideas for the wedding are _____.
   a. complicated   b. perfect   c. expensive

6. Marie wants Cheryl and Bob to _____.
   a. stop asking for help   b. say thank you   c. get back to work

Language in use

Excuse me.

People sometimes say **Excuse me** to call attention to an error. In this case, Marie thinks Bob and Cheryl have forgotten to thank her.

C What advice does Marie give to Bob and Cheryl? Complete the chart.

The size of the wedding	Plan a big wedding
The location of the ceremony	
The type of music at the ceremony	
The type of music at the reception	
The type of wedding cake	

Extend
These exercises will help improve your fluency.

Activate your grammar

Adjective clauses with subject relative pronouns

The reception should be held in a place **that is big enough for a large celebration.** (**The place** is big enough.)
It's believed that the woman **who** [or **that**] **catches the bride's flower bouquet** will be the next to get married. (**The woman** catches it.)

BE CAREFUL! Don't use a subject pronoun after a relative pronoun.
Don't say: The reception should be held in a place that ~~it~~ is big enough . . .
Don't say: The woman who ~~she~~ catches the bride's flower bouquet . . .

Subject relative pronouns
Use *that* for things
Use *who* or *that* for people

Plan a wedding **that's big enough to include all of Cheryl's family**.

D Complete each adjective clause with the subject relative pronoun *that* or *who*. Then draw an arrow from the subject relative pronoun to the noun that it describes.

1. Ann wants a wedding _____ is held outdoors.

2. The bride will wear a dress _____ was made in England.

3. The relatives _____ are coming from France will arrive a few days early.

4. Tim wants to hire the band _____ played at his brother's wedding.

5. The woman _____ will cater the wedding is supposed to be an amazing chef.

Activate your grammar

Adjective clauses with object relative pronouns

The music **that you choose** should appeal to guests of all ages. (You choose **it**.)
You should think carefully about the people **who** [or **whom**] **you invite to the ceremony**. (You invite **them**.)

Object relative pronouns
Use *that* for things
Use *who*, *whom*, or *that* for people

Note: An object relative pronoun may be omitted.
The music **you choose** should appeal to guests of all ages.
You should think carefully about the people **you invite**.

BE CAREFUL! Do not omit a subject relative pronoun.
The reception should be held in ~~a place is big enough~~ for . . .

E Use the cue to complete each adjective clause. Use *that* or *who* for subject relative pronouns. Omit any object relative pronouns.

1. The wedding ceremony should be held in a location _____.
   (The location is very beautiful.)

2. The reception should be in a place _____.
   (The place can hold a lot of people.)

3. People believe that the woman _____ will get married next.
   (The woman catches the bouquet of flowers.)

4. The "best man" is a friend _____ to hold the ring.
   (The groom chooses a friend.)

5. Plan a ceremony _____.
   (It combines traditional and contemporary features.)

6. I'd like to invite all the people _____.
   (I work with them at my company.)

7. The bride wants to wear the wedding dress _____.
   (Her mother wore it.)

8. The newlyweds went on a honeymoon _____.
   (Their colleagues paid for it.)

F Describe an ideal wedding, in your opinion. Use adjective clauses when possible.

Size of the wedding	
Location of the ceremony	
Location of the reception	
Type of music at the ceremony	
Type of music at the reception	
Type of food at the reception	
Activities right after the wedding	

Speaking option: Tell a classmate about your ideal wedding.

SCENE 2

running time — 1:56

Sneak peek: "Let's make today a holiday. We'll tell Mr. Evans we can't come back to work."

View — Read each exercise and then watch the video for the answers.

A Match each "holiday" with the person who introduces the idea.

___ 1. Paul   ___ 2. Mr. Evans   ___ 3. Bob   ___ 4. Marie   ___ 5. Cheryl

a. National On-Time Day
b. Red Day
c. National Wedding Day
d. National Buy-Your-Friend-Another-Cup-of-Coffee Day
e. National Singles Day

Language in use

Nice try.

People say **Nice try** to indicate that someone's attempt to trick them has not succeeded.

B Explain what happens on each of these "holidays."

National Singles Day	
Red Day	
National On-Time Day	

C Answer the questions.

1. Why does Paul come to the restaurant? _____
   _____

2. Why doesn't Bob want to go back to work? _____
   _____

3. Why doesn't Paul like the idea of National Buy-Your-Friend-Another-Cup-of-Coffee Day? ____
   _____

4. Why does Mr. Evans suggest celebrating National On-Time Day? _____
   _____

Extend
These exercises will help improve your fluency.

Expand your vocabulary

Ways to describe a holiday

historical: based on an event in history
seasonal: based on a time of the year
religious: based on people or events in religion
spectacular: very exciting to watch or participate in

D Choose two holidays you are familiar with. Explain the purpose of or reason for each holiday. Use adjective clauses when possible.

1. Name of Holiday: Harvest Fest
It's a seasonal holiday that celebrates the yearly harvest.

1. Name of holiday:

2. Name of holiday:

Expand your vocabulary

Ways to commemorate a holiday

set off fireworks   march in parades   have picnics   pray

send cards   give each other gifts   wish each other well   remember the dead   wear costumes

E Describe what people do on the two holidays you chose in Exercise D. Use adjective clauses when possible.

1. People give each other small envelopes that have money in them.

1.

2.

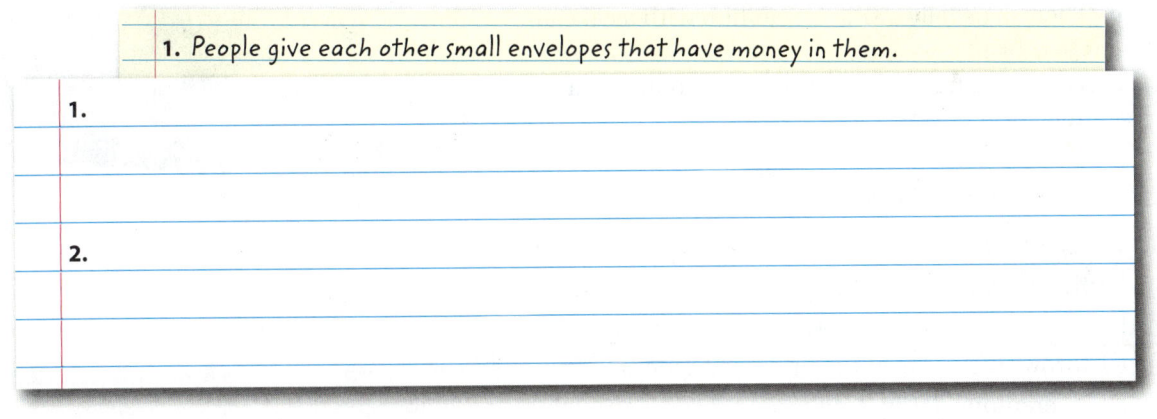

Speaking option: Describe a holiday to your classmates. Explain the holiday's purpose and what people do.

F Make up your own new holiday. Describe why it is celebrated and what people do.

Name of holiday:
Why it is celebrated:

What people do:

Speaking option: Tell a classmate about your new holiday.

41

ON-THE-STREET INTERVIEWS

Could you please describe a typical wedding in your country?

running time — 2:01

View
Read each exercise and then watch the video for the answers.

A Choose the correct description of weddings in each country.

Germany

1. a. There's usually one big ceremony.
   b. There are usually two ceremonies: civil and religious.
   c. There are usually three ceremonies: civil, traditional, and religious.

2. a. There isn't usually a reception after the wedding.
   b. There is usually a small reception with a cake only.
   c. There is usually a reception with a meal and a party.

Ghana

3. a. There's usually an American-style wedding.
   b. There's usually a traditional wedding.
   c. Some people choose an American-style wedding and others a traditional wedding.

4. a. There isn't usually a reception after the wedding.
   b. There is usually a small reception with a cake and speeches.
   c. There is usually a big reception with food, dancing, and speeches.

B Check the correct answers.

1. Which of the following are mentioned as wedding customs in Germany?
   - ☐ throwing flowers at the guests
   - ☐ throwing rice at the bride and groom
   - ☐ throwing flowers at the bride and groom
   - ☐ a ceremony at City Hall
   - ☐ a ceremony at a church
   - ☐ a ceremony at the bride's home

2. Which of the following are mentioned as wedding customs in Ghana?
   - ☐ throwing flowers at the bride and groom
   - ☐ throwing flowers at the guests
   - ☐ dancing down the aisle
   - ☐ walking down the aisle
   - ☐ wearing traditional African clothes
   - ☐ celebrating for more than one day

42 UNIT 5

Extend

These exercises will help improve your fluency.

C Compare wedding customs in your country with those in Germany or Ghana. How are they similar? How are they different?

Similarities

Differences

Speaking option: Discuss with a classmate how wedding customs in your country compare with those in Germany or Ghana.

D Write an e-mail to a friend, telling him or her about a wedding that you attended or in which you participated. Describe the ceremony, the reception, the food, etc. Explain in what ways the wedding was traditional or departed from tradition.

To:
Cc:
Subject:

43

TOP NOTCH POP SONG Endless Holiday
running time — 2:25

A Listen to the song "Endless Holiday." Then listen without looking at the screen and complete the lyrics.

Day after _____ 1.
all my thoughts drift _____ 2.
before they've begun.
I sit in my _____ 3.
in the darkness and _____ 4.
just waiting for someone
to take me to a tourist town,
with parties in the street and people
dancing to a joyful sound.

It's a song _____ 5.
It's the laughter _____ 6.
on an endless holiday.
It's the happiness _____ 7.
It's a roller coaster _____ 8.
on an endless holiday.

I try and I _____ 9.
to work hard, but _____ 10.
get lost in a daze,
and I think _____ 11.
how sad life is _____ 12.
a few good holidays.
I close my eyes, pull down the _____, 13.

and in my imagination I am dancing in a
big _____, 14.
and the music is _____. 15.
I get lost in the _____ 16.
on an endless holiday.
It's a _____. 17.
It's a trip to the _____ 18.
on an endless holiday,
with flags and confetti,
wild _____ and a great big 19.
marching band,
as we _____. 20.
in a language we all _____. 21.
The sky above fills with the _____ 22.
of _____ exploding, as we dance 23.
along the street _____. 24.

It's a song _____. 25.
It's the laughter _____ 26.
on an endless holiday.
It's the _____. 27.
It's a _____ 28.
on an endless holiday.

B What characteristics of a great holiday does the singer imagine?

_____
_____
_____
_____

44 UNIT 5

UNIT 6
I want to go someplace different.

Social Language
- Express fear of disasters
- Reassure someone
- Convey a message

Vocabulary
- Natural disasters and other emergencies

Grammar
- Direct and indirect speech

Preview
These exercises will help prepare you for the language in the video.

Expand your vocabulary

Natural disasters

a tornado

a hurricane / a typhoon / a monsoon

a flood

a landslide

a drought

They said on the news there's a monsoon in Thailand.

Other emergencies

an earthquake: the violent shaking of the surface of the earth that may cause damage or destruction to buildings and roads.

an epidemic: a quickly spreading outbreak of an infectious disease such as influenza

A Change the underlined words to make each statement correct.

1. In <u>a tornado</u>, the land is dry and animals and crops can't survive.

2. <u>An epidemic</u> is an event in which rocks and stones roll down hills, destroying many things in their path.

3. Cars were lost in the last <u>drought</u>, when the earth opened up and they fell in.

4. <u>An earthquake</u> is a whirling column of wind that can pick up houses and cars and blow them far from where they were.

5. In <u>a hurricane</u>, lots of people get sick.

6. In <u>a landslide</u>, water from rain-filled rivers rushes over the land, washing away and/or covering the land, buildings, and cities and towns.

7. <u>A landslide</u> is a severe storm with heavy rain and wind.

45

SCENE 1

running time — 2:43

> How about California? The Big Sur area is spectacular.
>
> California has lots of earthquakes, doesn't it?

Sneak peek

View Read each exercise and then watch the video for the answers.

A Match the place with the event Mrs. Beatty fears. One event is used twice.

___ 1. Thailand
___ 2. Australia
___ 3. Jamaica
___ 4. South Africa
___ 5. Hawaii

a.    b.    c.    d.

B Complete each statement.

1. Mr. Evans and Mrs. Beatty are trying to plan _____.
   a. a vacation for Mr. Evans
   b. a vacation for Mrs. Beatty
   c. a vacation in Asia

2. Mrs. Beatty wants to _____.
   a. take the same kind of vacation she always takes
   b. take a different kind of vacation from the ones she usually takes
   c. take a vacation in a major city in Europe

3. Mr. Evans says California has _____ earthquakes.
   a. occasional
   b. frequent
   c. severe

4. Mrs. Beatty heard that there was _____ in Thailand.
   a. a beautiful beach
   b. a bad storm
   c. an epidemic

5. Mrs. Beatty is afraid to go to Australia because of _____.
   a. the tornadoes
   b. the typhoons
   c. the droughts

6. Three other places Mr. Evans _____ are Jamaica, Hawaii, and Finland.
   a. warns Mrs. Beatty about
   b. suggests to Mrs. Beatty
   c. books tickets for

7. Finally, Mrs. Beatty decides _____.
   a. to go to Finland
   b. to go to Thailand
   c. not to go anywhere

C Mark each statement *T* (true) or *F* (false).

_____ 1. Mrs. Beatty's biggest concern is safety.

_____ 2. Mrs. Beatty doesn't want to go to California because she's afraid of the floods there.

_____ 3. Mr. Evans doesn't admit that California has earthquakes.

_____ 4. Mrs. Beatty finds something unsafe in all the places he recommends, except one of them.

_____ 5. Mr. Evans tries to reassure Mrs. Beatty about Thailand by telling her that the monsoon will be gone when she arrives there.

_____ 6. Mr. Evans tells Mrs. Beatty that Finland has a lot of natural disasters.

Language in use

But it **does** have earthquakes.

People use the auxiliary **do** or **does** to emphasize the main verb of the sentence when they want to contradict someone else's statement.

Extend
These exercises will help improve your fluency.

D Write an e-mail from Mrs. Beatty to a friend, telling her about the vacation she's going to take. Describe all the places Mr. Evans proposed before suggesting Finland.

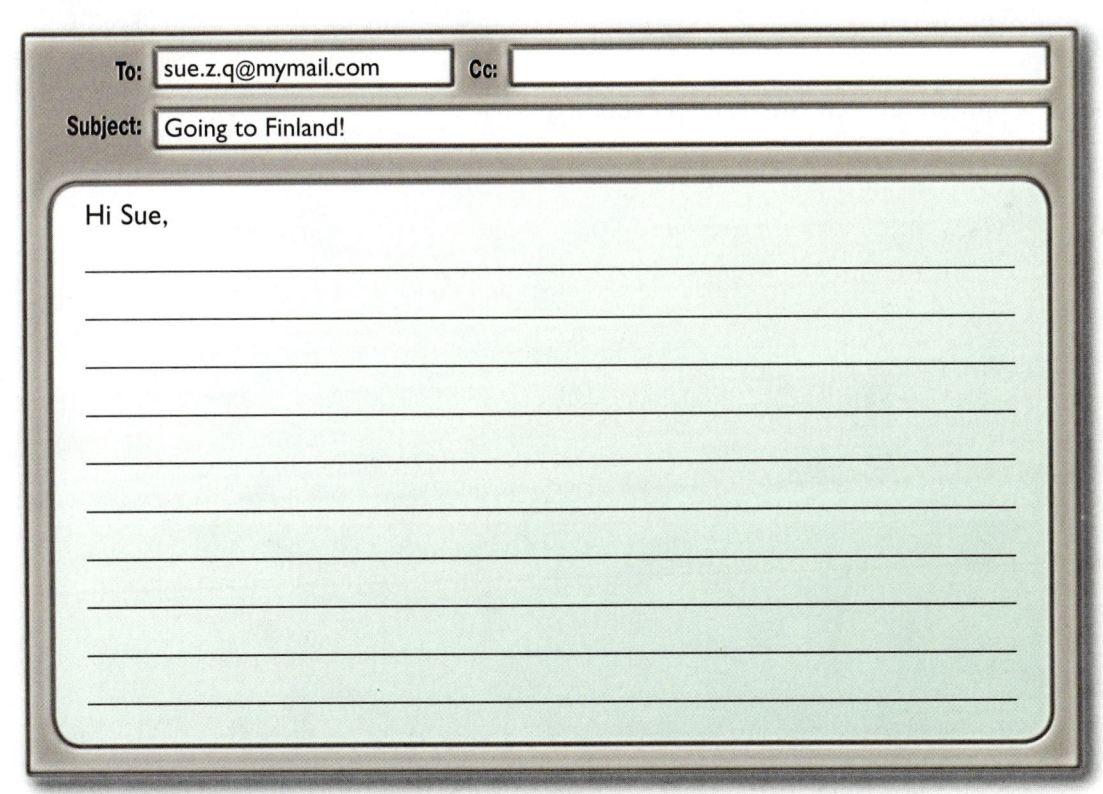

To: sue.z.q@mymail.com   **Cc:**
Subject: Going to Finland!

Hi Sue,

_____
_____
_____
_____
_____
_____
_____
_____
_____
_____

E Write a video script in which Mr. Evans suggests even more places for Mrs. Beatty to visit. Mrs. Beatty asks questions and voices her concerns.

> A: What about China?
> B: China? Don't they have typhoons there?
> A: Well, ...

🗣 **Speaking option:** Act out your video script with a classmate.

F Have you or has anyone you know ever experienced a severe weather event or an earthquake? Describe what happened.

Type of disaster:
Where?   When?
What happened?

🗣 **Speaking option:** Tell a classmate about your experience.

48   UNIT 6

SCENE 2
running time — 1:55

Sneak peek: I'm not going to Finland.

View — Read each exercise and then watch the video for the answers.

A Complete the scripts, according to what they say in the video.

1. OK. I just _____ to Helsinki, Finland. You _____ at the Palace Hotel.
   _____.

2. _____, Mr. Evans?
   Yes, Marie?
   Mr. Woods _____. He told me to tell you it's _____.

3. He said there's some kind of _____.
   _____?
   _____ it's that new influenza.

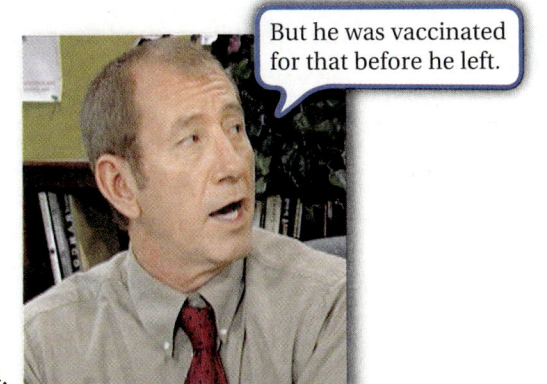

4. But he was vaccinated for that before he left.
   I know. But he _____ that he wants to fly home today.
   On the Internet it _____ _____ are sick.

49

B Complete each statement.

1. Mr. Evans has just _____ Finland.
   a. warned Mrs. Beatty about
   b. made reservations for tickets to
   c. gone to

2. Marie tells Mr. Evans that Mr. Woods _____.
   a. has influenza
   b. wants to speak to Mr. Evans
   c. doesn't want to go to Finland

3. Mr. Woods is afraid of _____.
   a. flying
   b. getting sick
   c. natural disasters

4. Mrs. Beatty says she _____.
   a. doesn't want to get vaccinated
   b. doesn't want to go to Finland
   c. doesn't want to be the first to die from the new influenza

5. Mr. Evans tries to tell Mrs. Beatty that _____.
   a. there's no epidemic in Finland
   b. he's not going anywhere
   c. nowhere is completely safe

C Read each false statement. Cross out and correct the false information to make the statement true.

1. Mrs. Beatty has a message for Mr. Evans.
2. Mr. Evans is calling Mr. Woods.
3. Mr. Woods wants to go to Finland.
4. Mr. Woods didn't get vaccinated for the flu.
5. Three hundred people in Finland are sick with the flu.
6. Mr. Evans says that Mrs. Beatty can't get vaccinated.
7. Mrs. Beatty decides she wants to go to Finland.

D Mr. Evans booked tickets for Mrs. Beatty to go to Finland. What happened to change her mind about the trip? Summarize the story.

_____
_____
_____
_____

Extend
These exercises will help improve your fluency.

Activate your grammar

Direct and indirect speech
Use quotation marks to write direct speech.
Marie said, **"Come home early."**

Don't use quotation marks to write indirect speech.
Marie said **to come home early**.

In indirect speech, an imperative becomes an infinitive.
Rose said, "**Come** home early." → Rose said **to come** home early.
Dan said, "**Don't go** to Ukraine this time of year." → Dan said **not to go** to Ukraine this time of year.

In indirect speech, make necessary changes in pronouns and time expressions to preserve the speaker's meaning.
They told Ila, "Call **us tomorrow**." → They told Ila to call **them the next day**.

Use *tell* when you mention the listener(s). Use *say* when you don't.
The announcer **told them** to wait for the weather report before leaving.
The announcer **said** to wait for the next weather report before leaving.

When *say* or *tell* is in a past tense, the verbs in the indirect speech statement often change. Present forms shift to past forms, and past forms shift to past perfect forms.
They said, "Finland **is** a great place to go." → They said that Finland **was** a great place to go.
Mr. Evans said, "**I'm going to book** your tickets." → Mr. Evans said he **was going to** book her tickets.
Mrs. Beatty said, "There **was** a monsoon in Thailand." → Mrs. Beatty said there **had been** a monsoon in Thailand.

E Circle the correct word or phrase to complete the instant messages.

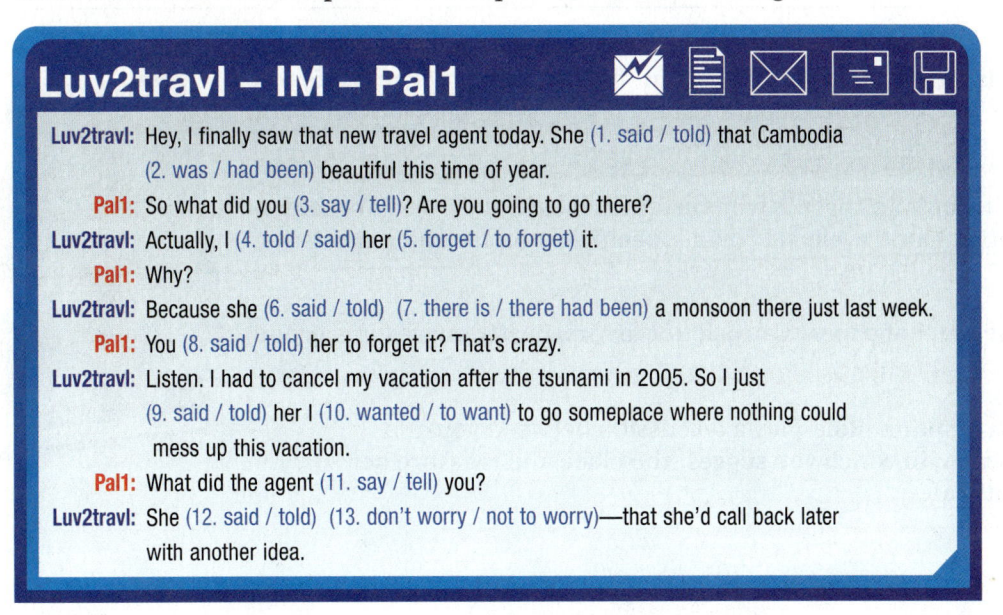

Luv2travl – IM – Pal1

Luv2travl: Hey, I finally saw that new travel agent today. She (1. said / told) that Cambodia (2. was / had been) beautiful this time of year.

Pal1: So what did you (3. say / tell)? Are you going to go there?

Luv2travl: Actually, I (4. told / said) her (5. forget / to forget) it.

Pal1: Why?

Luv2travl: Because she (6. said / told) (7. there is / there had been) a monsoon there just last week.

Pal1: You (8. said / told) her to forget it? That's crazy.

Luv2travl: Listen. I had to cancel my vacation after the tsunami in 2005. So I just (9. said / told) her I (10. wanted / to want) to go someplace where nothing could mess up this vacation.

Pal1: What did the agent (11. say / tell) you?

Luv2travl: She (12. said / told) (13. don't worry / not to worry)—that she'd call back later with another idea.

F Complete each statement by changing direct speech to indirect speech. Change verb tenses where appropriate.

1. The agent told the client, "Go to Puerto Rico for a beautiful beach vacation."
   She told the client _____

2. My cousin said, "I usually travel to major cities in the United States."
   He said _____

3. The travel agent said, "I'll call you tomorrow."
   The travel agent said she _____

4. My husband said, "We're not going to Europe this year."
   He said _____

5. Mrs. Beatty said, "A quiet beach sounds nice."
   Mrs. Beatty said _____

G Answer the questions. Use indirect speech.

1. What did Marie tell Mr. Evans? _____

2. What did Mr. Woods tell Marie to tell Mr. Evans? _____

3. Why did Mr. Woods want to come home from Finland? _____

4. What did it say on the Internet about the influenza epidemic? _____

5. What did Mrs. Beatty say about going to Finland? _____

H Mr. Evans tells Mrs. Beatty that nowhere in the world is completely safe. Do you agree with him? On a separate sheet of paper, explain your answer. Provide specific examples and reasons.

> **Speaking option:** Discuss why certain places in the world are safer than others for travelers. Provide specific examples and reasons.

I On a separate sheet of paper, write a letter to Mrs. Beatty, suggesting a good place to travel.

> **Speaking option:** Role-play a discussion between you and Mrs. Beatty, in which you suggest the place and reassure her about its safety.

TOP NOTCH POP SONG Lucky to Be Alive
running time — 2:06

A Listen to the song "Lucky to Be Alive." Then listen without looking at the screen and complete the lyrics.

Thank you for helping me to survive.
I'm really lucky to be alive.

When I was caught in a freezing snowstorm,
you taught me how to stay warm.
When I was running from a _____
                                 1.
with no place to hide,
you protected me from injury.
Even the world's biggest _____.
                              2.
has got nothing on me,
because you can go faster.
You keep me safe from _____.
                           3.
You're like some kind of hero—
you're the best friend that I know.

Thank you for helping me to survive.
I'm really lucky to be alive.

When the big _____ came
                  4.
with the pouring _____,
                       5.
they were saying that
a _____ loomed.
      6.
You just opened your umbrella.

You were the only fellow
_____.
       7.
You found us shelter.
I never felt like anybody cared
the way that you did when you said,
"_____—
       8.
you can bet your life on it."
And when the cyclone turned
the day into night,
you held a flashlight
and _____.
         9.
You called for help on your cell phone.
_____.
       10.
_____,
       11.
in times of trouble _____."
                          12.
They said _____.
                13.
It was beyond imagination.
_____—
       14.
and that is no exaggeration.

Thank you for helping me to survive.
I'm really lucky to be alive.

B Think about the meaning of the song. Then answer each question.

1. What's the main theme of the song? _____

2. What did the friend do for the singer during each of the following disasters?
   a. during a freezing snowstorm _____
   b. during a landslide _____
   c. during a big flood _____
   d. during a cyclone _____

3. What's the singer thankful for? _____

53

UNIT 7
May I ask you what you're reading?

Social Language
- Agree to lend someone something
- Describe reading material

Vocabulary
- Types of books
- Ways to describe a book
- Some ways to enjoy reading

Grammar
- Noun clauses: embedded questions
- Noun clauses as direct objects

Preview These exercises will help prepare you for the language in the video.

Expand your vocabulary

Types of books

FICTION

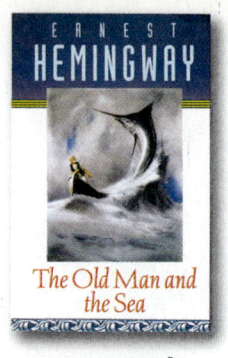

a. a novel
b. a mystery 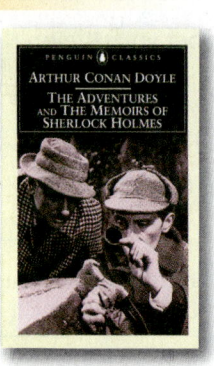
c. a thriller 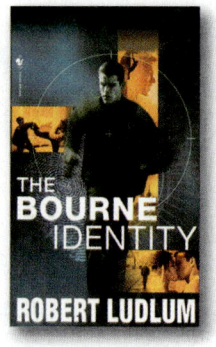
d. a romance novel  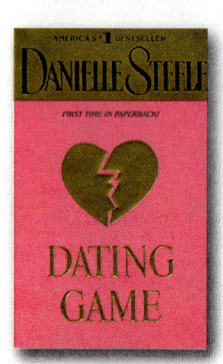
e. science fiction 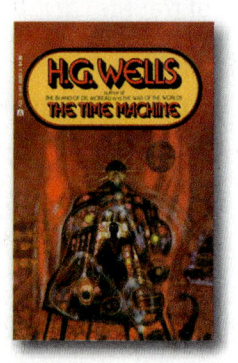
f. short stories 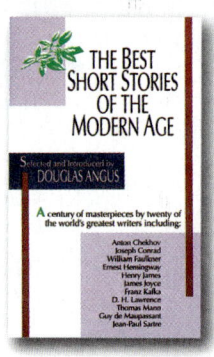

I usually prefer fiction myself. You know, thrillers, mysteries, ...

NONFICTION

g. a biography
h. an autobiography 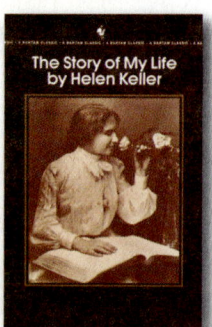
i. a travel book 
j. a memoir 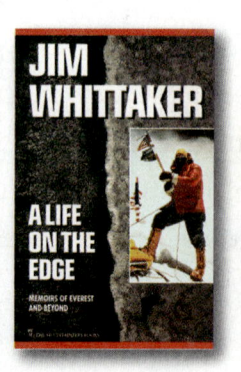
k. a self-help book 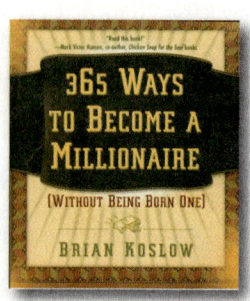

54 UNIT 7

A Read the book reviews and write the letter of the type of book.

_____ 1. Jerry Mundis keeps it simple with *How to Get Out of Debt, Stay Out of Debt, and Live Prosperously*, the foolproof guide to taking responsibility and setting things right again. Turn your life around.

_____ 2. By the year 2230, most people have accepted robots into their lives, trusting them to raise their children, perform daily chores, and fly their cars. But when scientist Jessica Miller discovers her robots talking behind her back on the sky bus, she suspects something is wrong—very wrong. *Robot Trouble* is a must-read.

_____ 3. You'd have to be from Mars not to have read something about Madonna's captivating and startling career. Finally, in *Material Girl Revealed*, we get to read the whole story in her own words. An eye-opening look into the life of one of the world's most popular superstars. Madonna tells all.

_____ 4. High among the rocky peaks of the Shawangunk Mountains, a peaceful family hike turns into a race of time and terror as Peter Benson tries to outsmart the mysterious men in green who claim to have kidnapped his wife and children. You'll keep turning the pages with one hand as you cling to your seat with the other. *Mountain Terror* is a real cliffhanger!

_____ 5. Nicole Santos does it again with *Technology to Riches*, a fascinating look into the life of Bill Gates, the world's richest man. As she did with the acclaimed *I. M. Pei: Architect of the World*, she takes us deep into the personality and private life of one of the world's best-known figures.

_____ 6. In *The Teahouse Murders*, the latest installment in the popular Judy Li series, Inspector Judy Li has good reason to worry. Another tea house owner has been murdered, and another message has been spelled out in tea leaves at the murder scene: "Number two. Stop me before I kill again." Who would do such a terrible thing? And why? A case only Judy Li could solve.

Do you mind **if I join you**?

Activate your grammar

Noun clauses: embedded questions
Begin embedded *yes / no* questions with *if* or *whether*.

Yes / no questions
Is it any good?
Have you finished the book?
Can I borrow it?

Embedded *yes / no* questions
I don't know **if** [or **whether**] **it's any good**.
Could you tell me **if** [or **whether**] **you've finished the book**?
I wonder **if** [or **whether**] **I could borrow it**.

Begin embedded information questions with a question word.

Information questions
What are you reading?
When was it written?

Who is the author?
Why don't you like this book?

Embedded information questions
May I ask **what you're reading**?
I'd like to know **when it was written**.
I wonder **who the author is**.
I can't understand **why you don't like this book**.

BE CAREFUL!
Use normal (not inverted) word order in embedded questions.
Do you know **who** the author **is**?
NOT Do you know ~~who is~~ the author?

55

B Rewrite each question as an embedded question. Use a question mark only if the rewritten text is a question.

1. Does he like to read a lot?
   Can you tell me _____

2. Where did she buy that new novel?
   I wonder _____

3. Does he prefer reading mysteries or thrillers?
   I don't know _____

4. Why do you read so many comic books?
   I'd really like to know _____

5. Who collected these short stories?
   I'm not sure _____

6. When did he start writing his autobiography?
   Could you tell me _____

SCENE 1
running time — 2:23

View Read each exercise and then watch the video for the answers.

Sneak peek
Cheryl hates when I read comics.

Language in use
Oh, **help yourself**.

People say **Help yourself** to indicate that it's OK for someone to borrow or look at something.

A Check the types of books Mr. Evans says he likes to read.

☐ comics
☐ travel books
☐ fiction
☐ mysteries
☐ thrillers
☐ self-help books
☐ romance novels
☐ short stories
☐ science fiction
☐ biographies

B Choose the best word or phrase to complete each statement.

1. Bob is waiting for _____.
   a. Mr. Evans
   b. Paul and Marie
   c. Cheryl

2. Mr. Evans asks Bob _____.
   a. what he's reading
   b. where Paul and Marie went
   c. where Cheryl is

3. Mr. Evans has heard that *A History of the World* is _____.
   a. easy to read
   b. expensive to buy
   c. hard to read

4. Mr. Evans wants to _____.
   a. borrow Bob's comic book
   b. borrow Bob's book
   c. buy a copy of Bob's book

5. Bob thinks Mr. Evans wants to _____.
   a. borrow his comic book
   b. borrow his book
   c. buy a copy of his book

C Complete Mr. Evans's embedded questions from the video episode.

1. **Bob:** Please, sit down.
   Mr. Evans: May I ask _____?

2. **Bob:** I can't put it down, actually.
   Mr. Evans: A real page-turner, huh? Do you think _____?

3. **Bob:** Uh, yes. I think so.
   Mr. Evans: So tell me _____.

4. **Bob:** Um . . . this part is about Great Britain.
   Mr. Evans: Really? Do you mind _____?

57

Extend

These exercises will help improve your fluency.

Expand your vocabulary

Ways to describe a book

- **a page-turner:** makes you want to keep reading it
- **a cliffhanger:** exciting; you don't know what will happen next
- **hard to follow:** difficult to understand
- **a bestseller:** very popular; lots of copies have been sold
- **a fast read:** not very challenging, but enjoyable
- **trash:** very poor quality

D Complete each sentence with the correct vocabulary word or phrase.

1. A: How's that book you've been reading?
   B: Oh, it's a real _____. I can't put it down!

2. A: Are you enjoying that new novel?
   B: Actually, it's kind of _____. I can't figure out what's going on.

3. A: I'm thinking about getting Watson's new thriller. Have you read it?
   B: I have. It's a real _____. I finished it in one weekend.

4. A: You just read *Love Affairs of the Rich and Powerful*, didn't you?
   B: I did. It's total _____—badly written and unbelievably silly. But I have to admit I still enjoyed reading it.

5. A: I highly recommend *The Spy Who Left Me*. It's really terrific.
   B: Oh, yeah. I heard it's a real _____. You keep wondering what's going to happen next.

6. A: Let me see what you're reading . . . *A Time to Fly*? Never heard of it.
   B: Where have you been? *A Time to Fly* is a _____. Everybody's reading it.

E Describe some of the books you have read. Use the vocabulary where appropriate.

Title of book	Type of book	Description
War and Peace	novel	a little hard to follow, but a real page-turner

Title of book	Type of book	Description

Speaking option: Tell the class about the books you've read.

58 UNIT 7

SCENE 2

running time — 1:49

It's in the paper. It must be true.

View
Read each exercise and then watch the video for the answers.

A Check the headlines Marie thinks are untrue or offensive.

- ☐ Storm Kills 100 in Texas
- ☐ A Man with Four Legs
- ☑ Baby with Two Heads
- ☐ Train Accident Kills Five, Injures More
- ☑ Woman Gives Birth to Cow
- ☑ Man Builds House From Bread
- ☐ Man Kills Wife and Son

B Who made each statement? Write *M* (Marie) or *P* (Paul).

_____ 1. "I'm not sure if you know this, but that story isn't true."

_____ 2. "That paper is trash."

_____ 3. "If you want real news, you have to read this paper."

_____ 4. "That paper is boring."

_____ 5. "All that death and destruction is pretty offensive to me."

_____ 6. "I know that these things happened. And I know that those didn't."

_____ 7. "Let's ask Bob and Mr. Evans what paper they read."

Language in use
Come on. This is offensive.

People say **Come on** when they disagree strongly with another person's opinion and want that person to change his or her opinion.

C Circle all the words that can complete each statement.

1. Marie believes that the stories in Paul's newspaper are _____.
   fiction   true   offensive   boring   interesting

2. Paul believes that the stories in his newspaper are _____.
   fiction   true   offensive   boring   interesting

3. Paul believes that the stories in Marie's newspaper are _____.
   fiction   true   offensive   boring   interesting

Extend
These exercises will help improve your fluency.

D Do you prefer the kinds of newspapers Marie likes or the ones Paul likes? Explain.

I prefer the kinds of newspapers Marie likes because ...

Speaking option: Tell the class whom you agree with and why.

Activate your grammar

Noun clauses as direct objects

A noun clause can be the direct object of a verb of mental activity.

                               noun clause
    I didn't know **that those stories weren't true**.
    I think **that some newspapers are just trash**.

Note: The word *that* can be omitted in noun clauses that are direct objects.
    I think ~~that~~ some newspapers are just trash.

As in reported speech, the tense in the noun clause often changes to support meaning.
    I hope we aren't too late. → I hoped we **weren't** too late.
    I think she finished the book. → I thought she **had finished** the book.

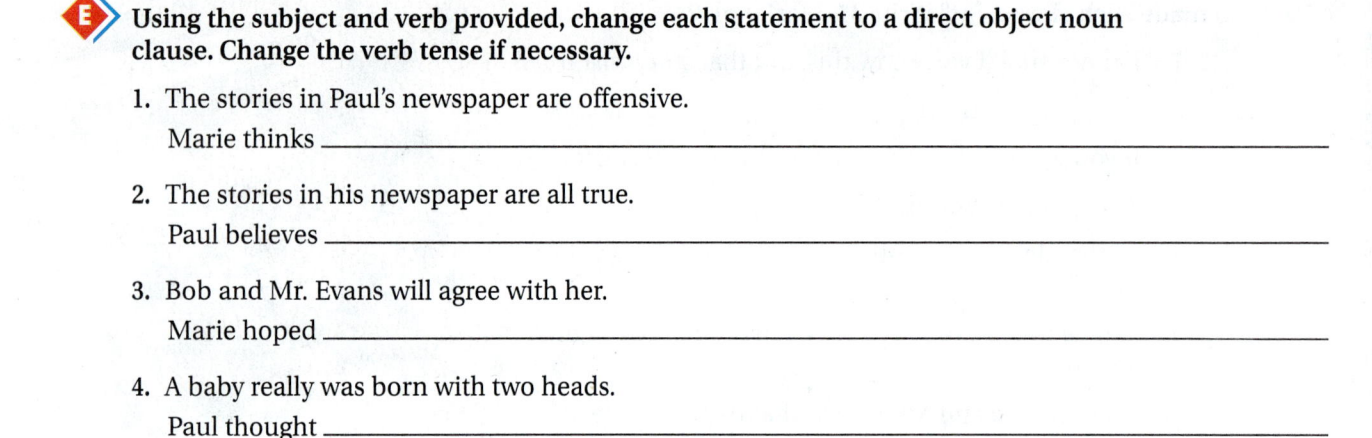

"Mental activity" verbs
think   believe
know   feel
hope   guess

E   Using the subject and verb provided, change each statement to a direct object noun clause. Change the verb tense if necessary.

1. The stories in Paul's newspaper are offensive.
   Marie thinks _____

2. The stories in his newspaper are all true.
   Paul believes _____

3. Bob and Mr. Evans will agree with her.
   Marie hoped _____

4. A baby really was born with two heads.
   Paul thought _____

5. Marie and Paul are never going to agree about this.
   I guess _____

F   Why do you think Bob and Mr. Evans don't want to respond when Marie asks what paper they read? Write your explanations, using the verbs *think, hope, know, believe,* or *feel* with noun clauses as direct objects.

> *Bob thinks that Marie will just be angry if they answer. He feels that...*

Speaking option: Tell the class why you think Bob and Mr. Evans don't want to respond.

60   UNIT 7

ON-THE-STREET INTERVIEWS

Do you do a lot of reading?

running time — 1:36

View

Read each exercise and then watch the video for the answers.

A Check the types of reading materials that are mentioned in the interviews.

- ☐ newspapers
- ☐ fashion magazines
- ☐ sports magazines
- ☐ how-to magazines
- ☐ car magazines
- ☐ mysteries
- ☐ travel books
- ☐ novels
- ☐ books on tape
- ☐ self-help books
- ☐ biographies
- ☐ science fiction

Language in use

Absolutely. I mean, belly laughs on every page.

People say **Absolutely** to strongly confirm that something is true.

B Choose the best word or phrase to complete each statement.

Blanche    Dan    Alvino    Lorayn

1. Blanche isn't crazy about _____.
   a. books on tape   b. mysteries   c. travel books

2. Dan is a fan of _____.
   a. nonfiction   b. fiction   c. fashion magazines

3. Alvino often reads _____.
   a. nonfiction   b. fiction   c. fashion magazines

4. Lorayn likes to buy her husband _____.
   a. newspapers   b. fashion magazines   c. how-to magazines

5. Dan's favorite parts of the newspaper are _____.
   a. the sports section and the "Arts and Leisure" section
   b. the front page and the "Home and Garden" section
   c. the front page and the "Arts and Leisure" section

61

C Mark each statement *T* (true) or *F* (false), according to the video. Then explain your answer.

_F_ 1. Blanche doesn't do a lot of reading.
   Both Herb and Blanche say that she does a lot of reading.

___ 2. Lorayn probably borrows a lot of books from the library.
   _____

___ 3. Blanche probably doesn't listen to books on tape anymore.
   _____

___ 4. The novel *How to Be Good*, by Nick Hornby, is probably a thriller.
   _____

___ 5. Alvino probably reads other things besides magazines.
   _____

___ 6. Lorayn probably likes to fix things around the house.
   _____

___ 7. Dan probably reads the sports page first when he buys a newspaper.
   _____

Extend
These exercises will help improve your fluency.

Expand your vocabulary

Some ways to enjoy books, magazines, and newspapers

curl up with a book

read aloud to someone

collect clippings

do puzzles

skim through a newspaper

listen to books on tape

D What are your reading habits? Answer the questions, using the vocabulary where appropriate.

What do you most like to read?
Who are some of your favorite authors?
Where do you usually like to read?
How do you read magazines and newspapers? (Do you: skim? read carefully? go to a section first?)

Speaking option: Tell a classmate about your reading habits.

Expand your vocabulary

Ways to talk about what you're reading

Positive	Negative
I can't put it down.	I can't get into it.
I'm really into it.	It doesn't turn me on.
I can't get enough of it.	

E Describe something you're reading now or something you've read recently. Complete one or both columns. Use the vocabulary where appropriate.

What are you reading now?	What have you read recently?
Are you enjoying it?	Did you enjoy it?
Would you recommend it to others?	Would you recommend it to others?
Explain:	Explain:

Ways to describe a book
a page-turner
a cliffhanger
hard to follow
a bestseller
a fast read
trash

Speaking option: Tell a classmate about something you are reading now or something you have read recently.

UNIT 8
Technology today is amazing!

Social Language
- Describe innovative products
- Offer advice

Vocabulary
- Ways to describe inventions and manufactured products

Grammar
- Factual and unreal conditional sentences

Preview These exercises will help prepare you for the language in the video.

Activate your grammar

Factual and unreal conditional sentences

Present factual conditionals: Use the simple present tense or the present of *be* in both clauses.

If you **have** TV glasses, you **don't have to** stay home when the game's on TV.

Future factual conditionals: Use the simple present tense or the present of *be* in the *if* clause. Use the future with *will* or *be going to* in the result clause.

If they **buy** the MX-1 picture phone, they **will be able to send** photos to their friends.

Present unreal conditionals: Use the simple past tense or *were* in the *if* clause. Use *would* in the result clause.

If you **went** to Shop Quick, you **would get** a better deal on that MP3 player.
If Bob **were** here, he **would show** us how to use this DVD player.

Past unreal conditionals: Use the past perfect in the *if* clause. Use *would have* + a past participle in the result clause.

If I **had read** the report, I never **would have bought** this new portable TV.

Note: The order of the *if* clause and the result clause can be reversed.
I never would have bought this new portable TV if I had read the report.

Bob's new TV glasses.

BE CAREFUL!
Don't use a future form in the *if* clause.

If they see a cell phone at a good price, they'll buy it.
NOT If they ~~will~~ see a cell phone ...

BE CAREFUL!
Don't use *would* in the *if* clause.

Present unreal conditional: If she knew which brand of glasses was the cheapest, she'd get that one.
NOT If she ~~would know~~ ...

Past unreal conditional: If they had bought a new TV, they wouldn't have bought the glasses.
NOT If they ~~would have bought~~ ...

64 UNIT 8

A Choose the word or phrase that completes each conditional sentence.

1. If you don't like to write letters, _____ a good idea to keep in touch with people by instant-messaging them.
   a. it's
   b. it will be
   c. it would be

2. You can get a good deal on a new computer if you _____ the Internet.
   a. will go on
   b. are going to go on
   c. go on

3. If people _____ reviews of new inventions before they bought them, they'd probably buy fewer new things.
   a. are going to read
   b. will read
   c. read

4. If I had known that my computer didn't come with a built-in DVD drive, I _____ it.
   a. wouldn't have bought
   b. wouldn't buy
   c. won't buy

5. Our family is going to buy another car if my wife _____ a job out of town.
   a. will get
   b. gets
   c. would get

6. If you don't have a cell phone, people _____ you anytime they want.
   a. can't reach
   b. wouldn't be able to reach you
   c. wouldn't reach

7. They would have been able to watch the football game in the car _____ a car with a wireless TV.
   a. if they would have gotten
   b. if they had gotten
   c. if they got

B Complete the conditional sentences with the correct form of the verbs. Use the words in parentheses.

1. If you _____ (try) my new computer, you'll definitely want to get one for yourself.

2. If you have the XR-7 MP3 player, you _____ (can) download songs very quickly.

3. We wouldn't have seen that movie if we _____ (know) how violent it was.

4. If they _____ (read) the movie review, they won't go to that movie.

5. If our car had a TV in it, our kids _____ (watch) movies on long trips.

6. We _____ (spend) less time cutting vegetables if we buy this new food processor.

7. She _____ (send) you an e-mail message if she could find her PDA.

SCENE 1
running time — 2:17

These are ultra-high-tech, top-of-the-line, state-of-the-art, cutting-edge TV glasses.

View — Read each exercise and then watch the video for the answers.

A Mark each statement *T* (true), *F* (false), or *NI* (no information).

____ 1. Marie has seen Bob's new glasses before.
____ 2. Bob is watching TV on the glasses.
____ 3. Bob is watching a basketball game.
____ 4. Bob's team won the game.
____ 5. Cheryl doesn't like Bob's watching TV on his glasses.
____ 6. Cheryl doesn't like Bob's speeding.
____ 7. Bob has a lot of accidents because of his speeding.
____ 8. Marie hates it when people speak loudly on their cell phones.
____ 9. Marie has glasses that make people speak more quietly on their cell phones.

B Complete the scripts, according to what they say in the video.

1. **Cheryl:** If I _____ how happy they _____ him, I _____ those glasses for Bob long ago.

2. **Marie:** You know, I wish _____ something that _____ people who talk on cell phones quieter.

3. **Cheryl:** If I _____ something, it _____ a thing for Bob's car that _____ automatically _____ him when he _____ over the speed limit.

4. **Cheryl:** He _____ so fast sometimes, but _____ slow down _____ pay.

66 UNIT 8

C Answer the questions.

1. What does Marie find unbelievable about the glasses? _____
   _____
2. Why does Bob laugh? _____
3. Why doesn't Cheryl object to the glasses? _____
4. Why does Marie object to people's talking loudly on their cell phones? _____
   _____
5. What does Cheryl think would happen if Bob had to pay each time he went over the speed limit?
   _____

Extend These exercises will help improve your fluency.

Language in use

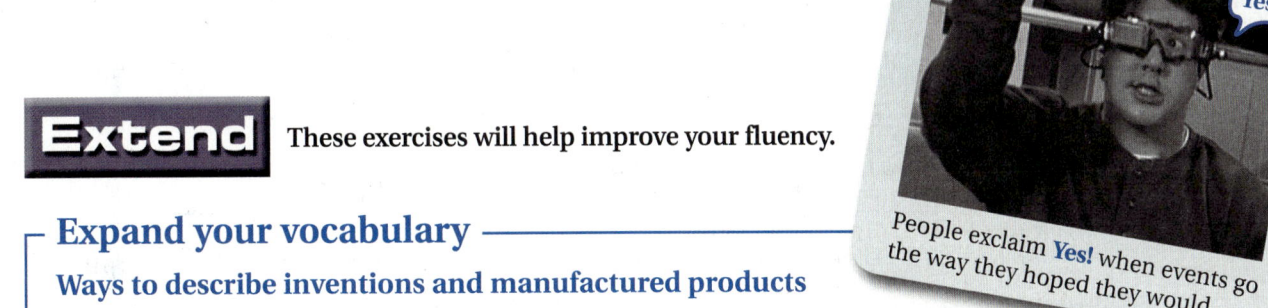

People exclaim **Yes!** when events go the way they hoped they would.

Expand your vocabulary

Ways to describe inventions and manufactured products

Uses new technology	Offers high quality	Uses new ideas
high-tech	high-end	innovative
state-of-the-art	top-of-the-line	revolutionary
cutting-edge	first-rate	novel

D List real products or inventions for each adjective. Then explain what makes those products or inventions revolutionary, cutting-edge, or top-of-the-line.

	Products	Explanations
Revolutionary		
Cutting-edge		
Top-of-the-line		

E Complete the following statement about an invention you would like to see. Explain the benefits of your invention. Use the vocabulary when you can.

> If I could invent one thing, it would be . . .

F Write a video script for a TV commercial for each of the products and inventions. Use the vocabulary when possible.

> **Bob's glasses:**
> Announcer: Introducing the amazing new TV glasses. These glasses combine cutting-edge technology with top-of-the-line picture quality to provide the viewer with the ultimate in private TV viewing.

Bob's glasses:

Marie's invention:

Cheryl's invention:

Your own invention:

Speaking option: Role-play a presentation in which you convince a classmate to buy one of the inventions.

68 UNIT 8

SCENE 2

running time — 2:08

I have this problem with my cell phone.

Sneak peek

View Read each exercise and then watch the video for the answers.

A Answer each of the following questions.

1. Why did Paul get a new device for his cell phone?
   a. so he can call people when he's traveling with a group
   b. so he can travel with a group
   c. so he knows when people are calling him when he's traveling with a group

2. What's special about the new device?
   a. It buzzes Paul when someone is calling.
   b. Paul buzzes it when he calls someone.
   c. It rings when someone is calling.

3. What happens when someone calls Paul?
   a. It doesn't work.
   b. It hurts.
   c. It makes a funny sound.

4. What does Marie suggest Paul do with the device?
   a. take it back to the store where he bought it
   b. call the store where he bought it
   c. try to use it in the car while he drives

5. How does Bob know that Paul will be all right?
   a. because Paul will turn off the phone
   b. because Paul will get used to the phone
   c. because Bob will stop calling him

B Complete the scripts, according to what they say on the video.

1. **Paul:** I got this thing that lets me know _____ _____.

2. **Paul:** Man, if I ever _____ that, _____ whenever my phone is ringing.

3. **Marie:** Paul. If I _____, I _____ that thing back to the store before you hurt yourself.

4. **Paul:** I'm going. _____ _____.

5. **Bob:** I'll stop _____.

69

C Complete each statement with the name of the correct character from the video episode.

Paul   Cheryl   Bob   Marie

1. _____ has had a problem receiving phone calls.
2. _____ wants to know how the new phone works.
3. _____ asks if it works.
4. _____ calls Paul on the new phone.

Language in use

Ow!

People say **Ow!** (or **Ouch**) to express pain.

Extend
These exercises will help improve your fluency.

D Write an e-mail from Bob to a friend, explaining the joke he played on Paul.

To: jimsmith@palnet.com   Cc:
Subject: You gotta hear this!

Hey Jim,
_____
_____
_____
_____
_____
_____
_____
_____
_____

*TTYL, Bob

***TTYL** = Talk to you later

Speaking option: With a classmate, role-play a phone call between Bob and a friend in which Bob tells his friend what he did to Paul.

E On a separate sheet of paper, write a video script in which Paul returns the phone to the store where he bought it. Paul and the sales clerk discuss the problems with it. The sales clerk does not want to take the phone back.

A: I need to return this.
B: What's the problem?
A: If I get a phone call, I get hurt!
B: Well, if you ...

70   UNIT 8

TOP NOTCH POP SONG — Reinvent the Wheel
running time — 2:48

A Listen to the song "Reinvent the Wheel." Then listen without looking at the screen and complete the lyrics.

You've got your digi camera with
the Powershot,
Four mega pixels and a memory slot
You've got your _____.
                      1.
_____ of your digi pet.
        2.
I got the digi dog and the digi cat,
the digi this and the digi that.
I hate to be the one to break the news,
but you're giving me the digi blues.

And you don't know
the way I really feel.
Why'd you have to go and
reinvent the wheel?

You've got your cordless _____ and
                                    3.
your _____,
        4.
and your Reflex Plus for the perfect shave.
It's super special, _____,
                          5.
with the latest new, _____ design.
                            6.
You've got your SLR and your LCD,

your PS2 and your USB.
I've seen the future and it's pretty grim:
they've used up all the acronyms.

And you don't know
the way I really feel.
Why'd you have to go and
reinvent the wheel?

I keep waiting for a breakthrough innovation:
something to help our poor communication.
Hey, where'd you get all of that _____
                                        7.
taste?
Your faith in progress is such a waste.
Your life may be _____,
                        8.
but you don't understand the human heart.

And you don't know
the way I really feel.
Why'd you have to go and
reinvent the wheel?

B Make each statement *T* (true) or *F* (false).

_____ 1. He's got a good camera.
_____ 2. He sends her pictures and e-mail.
_____ 3. She likes all the technology he has.
_____ 4. She thinks he really understands her and her feelings.
_____ 5. She is happy with him.

C *Challenge:* Answer these questions.

1. What does the singer think is the main problem with their relationship?
   _____

2. Why does she say that his faith in progress is such a waste?
   _____

UNIT 9
Can we please avoid discussing politics?

Social Language
- State an opinion
- Disagree politely about controversial issues
- Discuss politics

Vocabulary
- Global issues
- A continuum of political and social beliefs
- Ways to agree and disagree
- Some controversial issues
- Ways to express opinions

Grammar
- Non-count nouns for abstract ideas
- Verbs followed by objects and infinitives

Preview These exercises will help prepare you for the language in the video.

Expand your vocabulary

Global issues

poverty: lacking money or possessions

discrimination: unfairly treating one group of people, such as those of a particular race or religion, differently from another

corruption: dishonest behavior in government or business

terrorism: use of violence to obtain political demands

They should spend more money on fighting corruption.

A Write the correct global issue next to each example.

1. A car bomb goes off next to a disco filled with two hundred people, injuring at least fifty. _____

2. A public official gives a government contract to a company owned by his brother, even though other companies offered lower prices. _____

3. Approximately one-fifth of the world's population, over one billion people, earns less than US$1.00 a day. _____

4. An office manager interviews a woman who is well qualified but decides not to hire her because of her religious background. _____

Expand your vocabulary

A continuum of political and social beliefs

conservative: *adj.* preferring to continue to do things as they have been done in the past rather than risking changes (a conservative *n.*)

liberal: *adj.* supporting changes in political, social, or religious systems that allow more people to do what they want (a liberal *n.*)

moderate: *adj.* having opinions or beliefs, especially about politics, that are not extreme and that most people consider reasonable or sensible (a moderate *n.*)

radical: *adj.* supporting complete political or social change (a radical *n.*)

reactionary: *adj.* strongly opposed to political or social change (a reactionary *n.*)

What makes you think I'm radical?

You always want to change everything.

B Complete each statement with the appropriate vocabulary word.

1. Many considered the last prime minister to be quite _____ because he strongly opposed all change.

2. The new Secretary-General of the United Nations was chosen for her _____ views, which would allow her to work with members representing a broad array of political beliefs.

3. The voters chose a more _____ candidate who promised to protect long-held traditions and not make any major changes.

4. The new government says it intends to establish more _____ policies in health and education that will allow more choice and opportunity for all citizens.

5. The new political party was considered by many to be too _____ in its insistence on immediate changes in the constitution, election rules, and government organization.

C Choose one of the following topics to write about.

1. How would you categorize your political and social beliefs? Write a paragraph, using some of the vocabulary. Provide examples of your views on specific issues.

   OR

2. Choose a local or national politician. How would you categorize the political and social beliefs of that person? Provide examples of his or her views on specific issues.

SCENE 1
running time — 2:38

View
Read each exercise and then watch the video for the answers.

Can we please avoid discussing politics?

A Check the topics discussed in the video episode.

- ☐ education
- ☐ pollution
- ☐ poverty
- ☐ terrorism
- ☐ discrimination
- ☐ military spending
- ☐ corruption
- ☐ crime

Language in use

That's true. But I think we need to spend more money on the military.

That's one way to look at it. But maybe the world would be safer—and better—if we tried to eliminate poverty.

People use **That's true. But** or **That's one way to look at it. But . . .** to disagree politely.

B Write the correct name to complete each statement.

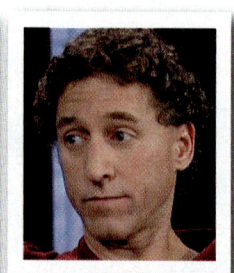

Bob   Paul   Cheryl   Marie

1. _____ thinks the government should do something about corrupt officials.
2. _____ thinks the government should spend more money on eliminating poverty.
3. _____ thinks the government should spend more money on the military.
4. _____ thinks people shouldn't talk about politics.

C Write the reason each person gives for the opinion he or she expresses in Exercise B.

1. Paul _____
2. Bob _____
3. Marie _____
4. Cheryl _____

74 UNIT 9

Extend

These exercises will help improve your fluency.

Some non-count nouns for abstract ideas
education, terrorism, peace, poverty, crime, progress, spending, pollution, justice, corruption, discrimination, health, racism

Activate your grammar

Non-count nouns for abstract ideas
Nouns that represent abstract ideas are non-count nouns.

Remember: Non-count nouns are neither singular nor plural. They have no plural form, and they are not preceded by *the*, *a*, or *an*.

Education is an important issue. { NOT ~~The~~ education is an important issue.
NOT Education ~~are~~ an important issue. }

D Complete each statement with the correct form of the nouns and verbs.

1. The government should spend more money to fight _____ and _____.
   crime / the crime *corruption / the corruption*
2. I think _____ _____ the greatest threat to progress in this country.
   poverty / a poverty *is / are*
3. The voters chose _____ who promised to make _____ her priority.
   candidate / the candidate *education / the education*
4. There should be an increase in _____ to improve _____.
   spending / the spending *health / the health*
5. _____ _____ one of the greatest problems facing _____.
   Discrimination / The discrimination *is / are* *world / the world*
6. Unless there is _____ for all, _____ will only increase.
   justice / a justice *terrorism / the terrorism*

E What issues do you think most need to be addressed in your country or in the world? Explain what you think should be done.

Issue	What should be done?
poverty	The government should spend more money on education so poor children can have more opportunities.

Issue	What should be done?

Speaking option: Tell a classmate your ideas about local and world issues.

F On a separate sheet of paper, write a video script in which a group of friends argue about a political or social issue.

A: I think poverty is the greatest problem the world faces.
B: Really? I'm not sure I agree. I think terrorism is a much bigger problem.
A: That's one way to look at it, but...

Ways to agree
I agree with you on that one.
I couldn't agree more.
I couldn't have said it better myself.
That's exactly what I think.

Ways to disagree
That's true, but ...
That's one way to look at it, but ...
I see what you mean, but ...
Really? I have to disagree with you there.
Do you think so? I'm not sure I agree.

SCENE 2
running time — 2:13

Sneak peek

Paul, I never knew you were so conservative.

View
Read each exercise and then watch the video for the answers.

A Complete each statement with *thinks* or *doesn't think*.

1. Paul _____ he's a conservative.
2. Paul _____ Marie's a radical.
3. Marie _____ she's a radical.
4. Bob _____ he's a liberal.
5. Marie _____ Bob's a liberal.
6. Marie _____ Bob's a moderate.

Language in use

I'm not conservative.
Sure you are.

People use **Sure you are** (or **do**) to contradict another person.

B Who's talking about whom? Write the names of the people to complete each statement.

Marie   Paul   Bob   Cheryl

1. "You always seem to want things to be just like they used to be."
   _____ is talking about _____.

2. "You always want to change everything."
   _____ is talking about _____.

3. "I wouldn't call you a liberal."
   _____ is talking about _____.

4. "You're always in the middle."
   _____ is talking about _____.

5. "You just can't be one thing and call it something else."
   _____ is talking about _____.

6. "You're like a little dictator."
   _____ is talking about _____.

7. "She's not saying."
   _____ is talking about _____.

76   UNIT 9

C Complete each statement.

1. Marie wants the government to realize that _____.

2. Marie says she knows something about the definitions of political beliefs because _____
_____.

3. Cheryl believes that _____.

Extend
These exercises will help improve your fluency.

Expand your vocabulary

Some controversial issues

censorship of books and movies

compulsory military service

lowering the driving age

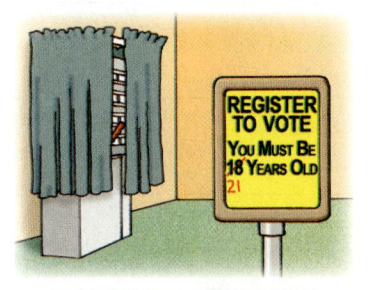

raising the voting age

prohibiting smoking indoors

your own controversial issue: _____

Activate your grammar

Verbs followed by objects and infinitives

Certain verbs can be followed by infinitives, but some verbs must be followed by an object before the infinitive.

The president **urged all citizens to vote** in the election.
They **warned everyone not to smoke** in public places.
The university **urged its students to take** part in the debate.

Verbs followed directly by an infinitive

agree	deserve	offer
appear	hope	plan
can't afford	learn	pretend
can't wait	manage	refuse
decide	need	seem

Verbs followed by an object before an infinitive

advise	invite	require
allow	permit	tell
cause	persuade	urge
convince	remind	warn
encourage	request	

77

D Using an object before the infinitive, change each sentence from the passive voice to the active voice. Use the phrase in parentheses as the subject of the sentence.

1. They should be told (by someone) to vote next week.
   Someone should tell them to vote next week.

2. Drivers need to be persuaded (by the government) to wear their seat belts.
   _____

3. Customers shouldn't be permitted (by restaurants) to smoke indoors.
   _____

4. The government should be urged (by people) to raise the voting age.
   _____

5. The library staff shouldn't be allowed (by the university) to censor books.
   _____

6. Students should be encouraged (by teachers) to participate in school affairs.
   _____

E What's your opinion? Complete each statement with *for* or *against*. Then explain your opinion.

1. I'm _____ censorship of books and movies.
   Reason: _____

2. I'm _____ compulsory military service.
   Reason: _____

3. I'm _____ lowering the driving age.
   Reason: _____

4. I'm _____ raising the voting age.
   Reason: _____

5. I'm _____ prohibiting smoking indoors.
   Reason: _____

6. I'm _____. (your own controversial issue)
   Reason: _____

Speaking option: Tell a classmate about your opinions.

ON-THE-STREET INTERVIEWS

running time — 1:43

How do you feel about . . . ?

View Read each exercise and then watch the video for the answers.

Language in use

I am **100 percent against** censorship.

People use **be 100 percent for** or **be 100 percent against** to emphasize how strongly they feel about an issue.

A Complete each statement with the correct name.

Ian   Christiane   Stephan

1. _____ thinks it's wrong to limit people's access to information.
2. _____ thinks it's important for people to communicate with each other.
3. _____ thinks it's a good idea to prohibit smoking indoors.
4. _____ isn't for prohibiting smoking indoors but understands why some people are for it.

B Choose the two correct answers to each question.

1. According to Christiane, what are some benefits of prohibiting smoking in restaurants?
   a. The food tastes better.
   b. Your clothes don't smell.
   c. You can breathe more clearly.
   d. The restaurant doesn't smell.

2. According to Stephan, what can be some results of censorship?
   a. It can make people less creative.
   b. It can create an atmosphere of fear.
   c. People might not be able to get the information they need.
   d. People might not be able to see the movies they want to.

3. According to Christiane, what are the biggest problems in the world today?
   a. racism
   b. air pollution
   c. smoking
   d. war

4. According to Christiane, what should be done to alleviate these problems?
   a. People should talk to each other more.
   b. People should try to understand other cultures.
   c. People should spend more money on education.
   d. People should stop smoking in restaurants.

C ▸ Complete the scripts, according to what they say in the video.

1. "As a smoker, I don't appreciate it all the time, but _____."

2. "I think _____. I think _____. If you go to restaurants and nobody can smoke, _____ and _____."

3. "I am 100 percent against _____ of _____ or any expression of creativity."

4. "I think actually with both problems it's _____ each other."

Extend
These exercises will help improve your fluency.

Expand your vocabulary

Ways to express opinions

I think / believe / feel …
   … it's wrong.
   … it's right.
   … it's OK, under some circumstances.
   … it's wrong no matter what.

D What do you think? Answer the interviewer's questions.

1. How do you feel about prohibiting smoking indoors?

2. How about censorship of books or movies by the government?

3. What do you think are the biggest problems in the world today?

4. What do you think could be done to alleviate these problems?

Speaking option: Discuss your answers with a classmate.

E Write a letter to Ian, Christiane, or Stephan, agreeing or disagreeing with a view they expressed in the video segment. Use the vocabulary and provide examples to support your opinions.

> Dear _____,
> I'm writing you this letter to tell you that I disagree with your opinion about . . .

81

UNIT 10
We weren't going to tell you this, but . . .

Social Language
- Warn about risks and dangers
- Describe the natural world

Vocabulary
- Geographical features
- Possible risks
- Positive and negative comments about places
- Dangerous animals and insects

Grammar
- Infinitives with *too* + an adjective

Preview
These exercises will help prepare you for the language in the video.

Expand your vocabulary

Geographical features

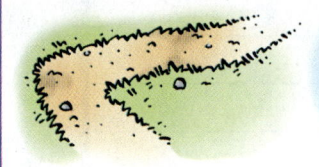

a path    a cliff    a cave    a waterfall    a beach

Possible risks

It can be quite **dangerous**.

It can be very **rocky**.

It can be extremely **steep**.

It can be really **foggy**.

It can be quite **slippery**.

It can be pretty **dark**.

It can be terribly **exhausting**.

82 UNIT 10

A Complete the e-mail with the vocabulary. Use each word once.

To: billmason@truenet.com **Cc:**
Subject: Today's adventure

Hi, Bill!

What an adventure we had today at the Cabo de Perros National Park! I wanted to explore the whole thing on foot, but they told me that a hike that long would be too _____ for a person my age! So I took a mule like everyone else and was I glad I did! They were right—I would
1.
have been very tired if I had walked. It's very mountainous, and the paths are incredibly
_____. I was scared we'd fall off the mountain! The paths are also very _____—
2.   3.
everywhere you step there are pieces of stone that have fallen. It would be really easy to trip over them. In the middle of the day, there was a heavy rain, and we had to take shelter in a very _____ cave—pretty scary! After the rain, everything got very _____, but the
4.   5.
mules were very sure-footed and not one of them fell. Even so, that trek was pretty _____.
6.
As the sun began to go down, it became cooler and really _____— it was hard to see more
7.
than a few meters ahead of us. By the time we got home it was pretty late, so we had to use flashlights. I guess we were lucky that no one was hurt, but we had fun!   —Natasha

---

Activate your grammar

Infinitives with *too* + an adjective
Use an infinitive after *too* and an adjective to give a warning or an explanation.
   It's **too dangerous to go** walking at night in that park. There's been a lot of crime there recently.
   The water at that beach is **too cold to swim** in.

Clarify with a *for* phrase.
   It's too dangerous **for you** to go walking at night in that park.
   The water at that beach is too cold **for most people** to swim in.

BE CAREFUL!
Don't say: The water is too cold to swim in it.

B Complete the answers to the questions about the trip described in Exercise A. Use *too* + an adjective and an infinitive.

1. Why did they tell her to take a mule?

   It would be _____ _____ for a person of her age _____ _____.

2. Why would it have been hard to walk?

   The paths were _____ _____ to climb and _____ _____ _____ walk on.

3. Why was it good to be riding mules after it rained?

   The paths were _____ _____ for people _____ _____ on.

4. Why was it so hard to get back to the hotel?

   It was very late and they had to use flashlights because it was _____ _____ _____ _____ more than a few meters.

SCENE 1

running time — 2:55

Sneak peek

"Stay in town? For our honeymoon?"

View Read each exercise and then watch the video for the answers.

A Complete the statements.

Mr. Evans   Paul   Cheryl   Marie   Bob

1. _____ and _____ want to know which places the others recommend for a honeymoon.

2. _____ wants to know if they're already considering a place.

3. _____ seems to care more about the hotel than the place.

4. _____'s first choice has always been to go to Cozumel.

5. _____ thinks Cozumel is a wonderful place.

6. _____ suggests that the sharks make it too dangerous to go in the water in Cozumel.

7. _____ changes his mind about Cozumel and says it's overrated.

8. _____'s next suggestion is Tierra del Fuego.

9. _____ comments on the beauty of the mountain ranges and the national parks there.

10. _____ then insists that it's definitely not too dark to go there in June.

11. _____'s next suggestion is Malaysia.

12. _____ admits that there may be a lot of scorpions there, making it too dangerous to hike.

a shark

a scorpion

84   UNIT 10

B **Choose the best answer for each question.**

1. What does Cheryl ask the others their opinion of?
    a. where she and Bob should go on their honeymoon
    b. whether she and Bob should go on a honeymoon after their marriage
    c. whether they could convince Bob that it's fun to travel

2. Who asks for opinions about Cozumel, Tierra del Fuego, and Malaysia?
    a. Marie
    b. Mr. Evans
    c. Cheryl

3. Who seems to be in favor of all the places?
    a. Mr. Evans
    b. Bob
    c. Paul

4. What might be the problem with swimming in Cozumel, according to Marie?
    a. sharks
    b. scorpions
    c. darkness

5. What might be the problem with going to Tierra del Fuego in June, according to Marie?
    a. It could be too dark to see the beautiful scenery.
    b. It could be unsafe.
    c. It might not be romantic enough.

6. What might be a problem with going to the rain forests in Malaysia, according to Paul?
    a. They're not romantic.
    b. They're too lush.
    c. There are scorpions in them.

7. Why does Bob want to stay in a hotel on Grand Street?
    a. because it's in town
    b. because he thinks Cheryl will like it
    c. because it has nice bathrooms and big televisions

C ▸ **Complete the scripts, according to what they say in the video.**

1. I've always wanted to go to Cozumel, _____ Yucatan Peninsula.

   Cozumel is _____. The island itself _____, but the beaches are _____ and _____.

2. Aren't there _____ _____?

   No! It's very safe. What? Oh! But _____.

3. The scenery is _____! The mountain ranges and national parks are _____.

   But in June won't it be _____ _____?

4. I've heard the jungles and rain forests in Malaysia _____.

   They're _____ . . . Of course, some people feel that the _____ _____.

86　UNIT 10

Extend These exercises will help improve your fluency.

> **Expand your vocabulary**
>
> **Positive and negative comments about places**
>
> | Positive | Negative |
> |---|---|
> | It's a must-see. | It's overrated. |
> | You don't want to miss it. | It's a waste of time. |
> | The scenery is breathtaking. | |
> | The views are spectacular. | |
> | The sights are extraordinary. | |

D Describe what you think would be an ideal honeymoon location for Cheryl and Bob, based on what you know about each character. Explain your choice.

_____
_____
_____

E Write a video script for a breakfast conversation between Bob and Cheryl on their honeymoon in Tahiti, in which they decide how to spend the day.

> Cheryl: Let's go to the beach today. It's really spectacular.
> Bob: OK. But I think there are too many sharks to go swimming...

🗣 **Speaking option:** Act out your video script with a classmate.

F Write an e-mail from Cheryl to her mother, telling her about the conversation in the café and how she feels about planning the honeymoon. Then, on a separate sheet of paper, write Cheryl's mother's response.

| To: | m.morris@chatnet.com | Cc: | |
| Subject: | Guess what? | | |

_____
_____
_____
_____
_____
_____
_____
_____

🗣 **Speaking option:** With a classmate, role-play a phone conversation between Cheryl and her mother.

SCENE 2

running time — 2:04

Sneak peek

"Thank you so much! I'm so excited!"

View Read each exercise and then watch the video for the answers.

A Read each false statement. Cross out and correct the false information.

1. Marie once told Cheryl she'd like to go to Tahiti.
2. Mr. Evans doesn't think Cheryl would like Tahiti.
3. Cheryl tells Bob that a trip to Tahiti would cost too much.
4. Mr. Rashid's trip to Tahiti was inexpensive.
5. Mr. Evans, Paul, and Marie give up because they're out of ideas.
6. Cheryl and Bob have to go someplace boring.
7. The group gives Cheryl and Bob a big TV for a wedding present.

B Choose the best answer for each question.

1. How does Marie know Cheryl wants to go to Tahiti?
    a. Cheryl once told her.
    b. Bob once told her.
    c. She guessed.

2. Which people think Tahiti would be a perfect choice for a honeymoon?
    a. Paul, Marie, and Mr. Evans
    b. Bob and Mr. Evans
    c. Marie and Mr. Rashid

3. According to Bob, what's the problem with a Tahiti honeymoon?
    a. It's very romantic.
    b. It's very expensive.
    c. It's very boring.

4. Why does Cheryl think they can't go to Tahiti?
    a. They haven't booked tickets.
    b. Bob won't be able to get the kind of hotel room he wants.
    c. They won't be able to afford it.

5. What makes their Tahiti honeymoon a reality?
    a. a cheap hotel on the southern coast
    b. a gift from the group
    c. Bob decides to pay for it.

C Complete the scripts, according to what they say in the video.

1. Cheryl, you once told me _____ _____.
That's right. I _____.

2. Well, do you remember _____?
_____.
He traveled _____.

3. Well, that's it. I'm _____. I guess _____.
We _____ until a couple of months from now, but Paul, Marie, and I _____, and _____ a vacation in the South Pacific _____.

4. So we decided that as our wedding gift to you, _____ _____. All expenses paid.
_____!

Extend
These exercises will help improve your fluency.

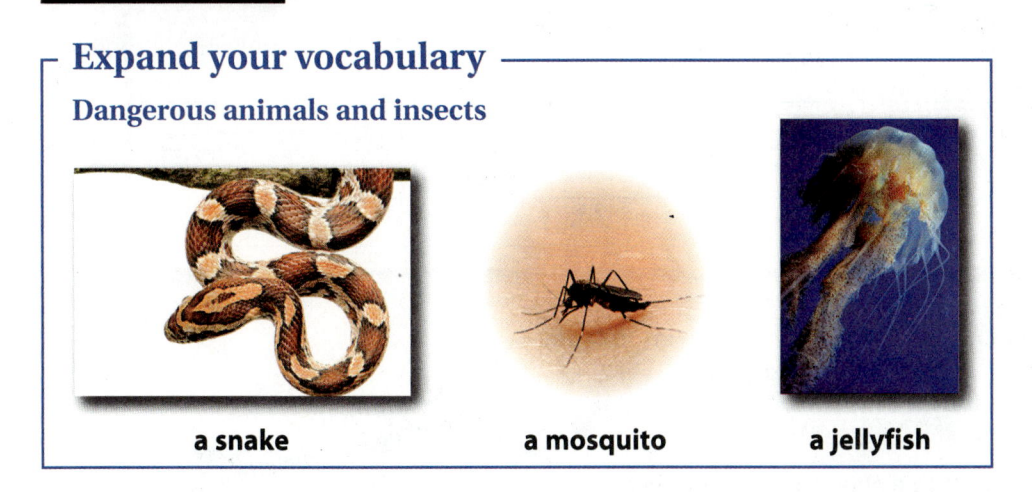

Expand your vocabulary

Dangerous animals and insects

a snake **a mosquito** **a jellyfish**

89

D Read the newspaper ad for adventure vacations. Then write the pros and cons of each vacation. Use the vocabulary and your own ideas.

Adjectives
dangerous
dark
exhausting
foggy
rocky
slippery
steep

Positive and negative comments
It's a must-see.
You don't want to miss it.
The scenery is breathtaking.
The views are spectacular.
The sights are extraordinary.
It's overrated.
It's a waste of time.

TRAVEL
VACATION PACKAGES

Vacation Package 1
African safari
- Trek across the Serengeti
- Sleep under the stars
- Get close to all the animals

Vacation Package 2
Sail and swim in the South Pacific
- Couples only
- No guides
- Very romantic!

Vacation Package 3
Rock climbing and cliff diving from hidden Mediterranean coastal villages
- Only for the brave
- Swimming certification required
- Complete helicopter medical evacuation plan included

Vacation package 1
Pros:

Cons:

Vacation package 2
Pros:

Cons:

Vacation package 3
Pros:

Cons:

E On a separate sheet of paper, write about the vacation packages. Use the pros and cons from Exercise D. Use *too* + an adjective and an infinitive.

The African safari is a must-see. The animals are too incredible to miss.

Speaking option: With a classmate, role-play a discussion between a nervous tourist and a travel agent. Discuss one or more of the vacation packages. Decide which one to take.

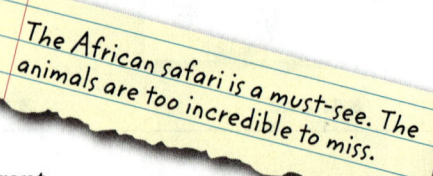

90 UNIT 10

Video Scripts

Video scripts

Unit 1

Sitcom

Scene 1

Cheryl: Marie, can I have that information for Mr. Rashid's group? He'll be here in a few minutes.
Marie: I'm working as fast as I can. *(to Mrs. Beatty)* Mr. Evans will be with you very soon.
Mrs. Beatty: That's fine. I'm a little early, aren't I?
Marie: Just a few minutes.
Mrs. Beatty: Is your last name pronounced "Le-PAIGE"?
Marie: It's "Le-PAHGE," actually.
Mrs. Beatty: Oh, that's beautiful.
Marie: Thank you.
Mrs. Beatty: Now, is it Ms. LePage or Mrs. LePage?
Marie: Um, it's Ms., but you can call me by my first name.
Mrs. Beatty: Do you mind if I call you Ms. LePage? I love the way it sounds.
Marie: That's fine.
Mrs. Beatty: I'm keeping you from your work, aren't I?
Marie: I'm sorry. I'd love to talk, but I really have to get this done right away.
Mrs. Beatty: I understand. You're not from here, are you?
Marie: Excuse me?
Mrs. Beatty: Your accent. You come from France, don't you?
Marie: Yes. Paris, actually.
Mrs. Beatty: That's nice. It sure is a beautiful day, isn't it?
Marie: Mmm-hmm.
Cheryl: Can I have that information?
Marie: I'm not quite done.
Cheryl: What's taking so long? *(to Mrs. Beatty)* Mrs. Beatty, I can take you to Mr. Evans's office. He'll be here shortly.
Mrs. Beatty: Why, thank you. Beautiful day, isn't it?
Cheryl: Yes, it is.

Scene 2

Mr. Evans: Paul, we have our first group from India coming next week. Since Mr. Rashid has traveled to India many times, I've asked him to talk to you about etiquette in India. Mr. Rashid?
Mr. Rashid: Paul, why don't you greet me as if I were an Indian tourist? Ask me to come with you and show me to the tour bus.
Paul: OK. Hi, there! I'm Paul.
Mr. Rashid: If I were an Indian woman, you would have just insulted me. Women and men generally do not touch.
Paul: OK. Uh, hi, there.
Mr. Rashid: You just told me to go away.
Paul: Oh, I'm sorry.
Mr. Rashid: Oh, too close. You should stand this far away from someone. Instead of shaking hands, do this and say "Namaste."
Paul: Namaste.
Mr. Rashid: Excellent. Now tell me to come with you to the tour bus.
Paul: OK. Come with me.
Mr. Rashid: This is a rude gesture in India. Do it like this.
Paul: Come with me.
Mr. Rashid: Good.
Paul: . . . to the bus over there. I know. I've just insulted you.
Mr. Rashid: Pointing with your fingers is considered impolite. Use your chin instead.
Paul: . . . to the bus over there. I'm never going to get this.
Mr. Rashid: You're doing wonderfully.
Paul: Oh, thank you, Mr. Rashid.
Mr. Rashid: Oh, too close.

Unit 2

Sitcom

Scene 1

Cheryl: Let's get Ms. Novak's tickets ready. She may be stopping by this afternoon.
Marie: Paul, are you OK?
Paul: No. I feel awful.
Cheryl: What's wrong?
Paul: I've got this horrible cold. I'm sneezing, and my back is killing me. I've got this pain in my hip. My neck has been bothering me all day. And I have a stomachache.
Marie: You may have to go see a doctor.
Paul: No! I hate doctors.
Cheryl: I wonder what could be wrong?
Bob: Maybe he's allergic to work.
Paul: I'm not kidding here. I'm in pain.
Bob: I used to want to be a doctor, you know. Say "Ahhh."
Paul: Ahhh-choo!
Bob: Now I remember why I didn't become a doctor.
Cheryl: Paul, you really must get some medical help.
Bob: A little acupuncture might help you feel better.
Paul: Stay away from me.
Cheryl: Dr. Anderson is meeting Mr. Evans downstairs in the café. Should we ask her to come up? She may be able to help.
Marie: Great idea. I'll go get her.
Bob: You might prefer an herbal remedy.
Paul: Stop it.

Cheryl: How long have you been feeling this way?
Paul: I got the cold last night, and the pain in my back started this morning.
Bob: Want to try a little spiritual healing?
Paul: You're making me laugh.
Bob: Laughter is the best medicine, you know.
Paul: But it hurts!

Scene 2

Dr. Anderson: Say "Ahhh."
Bob: Cover your face, doc.
Paul: Ahhh.
Dr. Anderson: Well, you have a cold, that's for sure.
Cheryl: What about the other stuff? The pain in the back and the side . . . ?
Dr. Anderson: Have you taken any medications lately?
Paul: Just some over-the-counter stuff—painkiller, cold tablets, nasal spray.
Dr. Anderson: That sounds OK.
Paul: And some cough medicine, vitamins, antacid.
Dr. Anderson: That's a lot of medicine.
Paul: And some decongestant.
Dr. Anderson: That's too much medicine in one day.
Marie: That must be why you're feeling so bad.
Dr. Anderson: Have you been around anyone else who's sick?
Paul: My friend Don has had a cold all week. We lifted weights last night for about an hour and ran five miles. He had to walk the last mile.
Dr. Anderson: Is that your usual exercise routine?
Paul: Yep. I started it yesterday.
Dr. Anderson: Well, that explains it. You exercised too much.
Paul: That's all?
Dr. Anderson: That's all.
Bob: A little chiropractic treatment might help you.
Paul: Stay away from me!

On-the-Street Interviews

Interviewer: Are you traditional in your medical ideas? That is, do you kind of believe in Western medicine, or do you like to explore nontraditional treatments, such as acupuncture or homeopathic medicine?
Joe: I don't explore nontraditional treatments as much as I would probably like to. I think there's probably a lot of merit in them, and they haven't been studied enough.
James: I'm more traditional than anything else in my medication, in my medical practices.
Vanessa: I'm more for the naturalistic approach. I like, you know, more natural herbal medicines.
Interviewer: In your opinion, what are the advantages of traditional Western medicine and surgery?
James: I think the enormous amount of research and . . . and . . . proven fact that's behind our medicine just makes it . . . makes me feel more comfortable with it.
Interviewer: What do you see as maybe some disadvantages of Western medicine?
Joe: I think at times Western medicine can make the problem worse than trying to make the problems better.
Interviewer: Are there any nontraditional therapies that you use?
Lisa: I drink a lot of tea actually, so I guess that's pretty nontraditional.
Vanessa: Usually when I feel myself coming down with something, I will take an echinacea, which is an herbal medicine. I'll probably drink a lot of orange juice because vitamin C helps you. But if I feel really sick, then I'll take cough medicine.

Unit 3

Sitcom

Scene 1

Mr. Evans: Now, about the travel documents for the Australian group. We've had everything mailed to them, right?
Cheryl: Mr. Evans, we gave you the package of travel documents to give to Mr. Wells the other night at dinner, before he flew home to Sydney.
Mr. Evans: A white envelope about this big?
Cheryl: Yes.
Mr. Evans: I gave it to Mr. Rashid before he left for Lebanon.
Cheryl: Oh, Mr. Wells needs those documents the day after tomorrow! His group is flying in on Thursday.
Marie: I'll call the courier. If they can pick up a package by 5:00 P.M., we should be OK.
Paul: That gives us an hour. I'll reprint the tour information, but what about the travel guides? I can't print twenty-five copies that fast.
Cheryl: I'll call Copies To Go and have them reprint the travel guides.
Marie: They can't do a rush job. Call Harper's instead. They're faster and much more reliable. *(on the phone)* Hello, National Express? I need to get a package to Australia a.s.a.p.
Paul: If Harper's can't make the color copies that fast, we'll take black and white.
Cheryl: Bob, are you reprinting the tickets?
Bob: Yep.
Cheryl: *(on the phone)* Hello. I need to get twenty-five color documents printed right away.
Mr. Evans: *(on the phone)* Yes, it's very much a hurry.
Cheryl: Who are you calling, Mr. Evans?
Mr. Evans: What's that? Oh, uh . . . my tailor.
Cheryl: Your tailor?
Mr. Evans: These sleeves are too long, and they're driving me crazy.

Scene 2

Mr. Evans: Thank you, everyone, for fixing my mistake with Mr. Wells. Now. I've asked Cheryl to plan a party for his group next Friday. I'd like for everyone to help. Cheryl, do you have a plan?
Cheryl: Yes, I do. Marie, I'd like to have you choose a restaurant for the party.
Marie: I'd love to!
Cheryl: Bob, I'll let you choose the menu.
Bob: You will?
Cheryl: Paul, could you plan the music?
Paul: Yes!
Cheryl: Good. Now, Marie, I called ten restaurants and had them give us a price for a party room. These two had the best prices.
Marie: The Green Room is a nice restaurant.
Cheryl: Great! That's my favorite, too. Now, Bob, about the food . . .
Bob: I was thinking steak, and potatoes, and . . .
Cheryl: Well, the client asked for fish or chicken. So I had the restaurant put together a menu with each. Which do you like better?
Bob: I like chicken more than fish, I guess.
Cheryl: Great! Chicken it is. Now Paul . . .
Paul: Let me guess. You have a list of music choices.
Cheryl: Yes!
Paul: These look fine.
Cheryl: Great! I think we're all done.
Mr. Evans: You see how easy it is to plan something when we do it all together?
Marie: So glad we could help.

Unit 4

Sitcom

Scene 1

Marie: Another wonderful dinner, Cheryl. Thank you.
Cheryl: You're welcome. I really enjoy cooking, actually. When I was young, I thought I was going to be a chef.
Paul: You could be a chef. These cookies are fantastic!
Marie: Why didn't you become a chef?
Cheryl: My mother talked me out of it. She thought I would always have to work at night. She was afraid I would never meet a man and get married.
Paul: She was probably right. If you were a chef, you wouldn't have met Bob.
Cheryl: How do you know?
Paul: Before he met you, Bob only ate fast food.
Bob: It's true.
Mr. Evans: Your mother must have been very happy when you and Bob got engaged.
Cheryl: She was. Hey, you'll never guess what Bob was going to be.
Bob: Cheryl . . .
Marie: A rock musician?

Paul: A basketball player?
Cheryl: No, Bob was going to be a dancer. He was actually in the state ballet when he was young.
Marie: No kidding!
Paul: You never told me this!
Bob: I could have been a great dancer.
Paul: What made you change your mind?
Bob: The diet was too hard. I had to stop eating everything—chocolate cake, fried chicken, potato chips. I tried. I might have been able to do it. But then they said no more bread and butter. Bread and butter! Can you believe it? And that was the end.
Marie: Wow, Bob. I never knew. Do you enjoy watching ballet at all?
Bob: I can't. I'd like to, but as soon as the music starts, I get very, very . . . hungry.

Scene 2

Marie: What about you, Mr. Evans? What did you think you were going to be when you were younger?
Mr. Evans: If I tell you, will you try not to laugh?
Marie: Of course.
Mr. Evans: I always thought I would have my own television program to talk about etiquette.
Cheryl: I didn't know you were so interested in etiquette.
Mr. Evans: I have always loved etiquette. I think I would have made a great television etiquette teacher.
Cheryl: Well, I think you could still do it. It's perfect for you.
Mr. Evans: Really? Why?
Cheryl: Well, you're very polite, for one thing.
Bob: You always know which fork to use at a restaurant. That's a real talent.
Paul: You've taught me a lot about the customs of other cultures.
Mr. Evans: Maybe I could still give it a try. "Today's topic: dinner conversation. If your international guests look offended and are leaving the table early, you've probably chosen a topic that's taboo in their home country. Find out what's acceptable and what's not . . . coming up on *International Etiquette with Evans.*" What do you think?
Bob: Wow.
Cheryl: Amazing.
Marie: Unforgettable.
Paul: You have a real . . . talent all right.
Mr. Evans: Thank you.

On-the-Street Interviews

Interviewer: Could you tell me what your career or occupation is?
Rita: I'm an elementary school teacher.
Matt: My career path will be in marketing, helping companies build their brand and help market products to the general consumer.

San: I work in television, and I would like to eventually produce and direct.
Interviewer: Did you think that you'd be in marketing when you were a child?
Matt: No. I thought I'd be president of the United States or drive a fire truck.
Interviewer: What made teaching a good career for you?
Rita: First of all, I love children, and I liked the idea of imparting some of my knowledge to young ones.
Interviewer: Everybody has skills, talents and abilities, so, you know, some people are artistic, others have mechanical ability. What would you say are some of your skills?
San: I would say I have a lot of artistic ability. I did a lot of art in school.
Matt: Good question. My skills and talents would be coming up with new ideas, different ideas, creative ideas that kind of build a buzz around a product.
Interviewer: Do you think that talents and abilities are genetic?
San: I think they're a combination of both genetics and environment. I think that you are born with certain qualities that your parents I think have, and just living with some people around you and learning from your teachers and those that you're constantly interacting with, you pick up certain skills.

Unit 5

Sitcom

Scene 1

Bob: I don't know. I didn't know that planning a wedding would be so hard.
Cheryl: Marie, could you give us your opinion on a few things?
Marie: I'd love to!
Cheryl: First, how many people should we invite? Bob wants a small wedding.
Bob: Twenty guests would be nice.
Cheryl: I want a large wedding. About 300 people.
Bob: Three hundred?! Yesterday you said 200!
Cheryl: I have a lot of relatives who want to come.
Bob: Then there's the location. I always thought I would get married in a park or at the beach.
Marie: That's so romantic!
Cheryl: I would like to get married indoors, where I won't get wet if it's raining.
Marie: That makes sense.
Cheryl: I prefer traditional music in the ceremony.
Bob: Contemporary music.
Cheryl: I'd like a long ceremony, and a short reception.
Bob: I want a short ceremony, and a huge celebration afterwards.
Cheryl: I want a white cake.
Bob: And I want . . .
Marie: A chocolate cake, I know.

Bob: How are we ever going to agree on this?
Marie: Don't hurt yourself. Here's an idea that might work. Plan a wedding that's big enough to include all of Cheryl's family . . . sorry, Bob . . . in the park on Oak Street that has that building where you can go if it rains. You can have traditional music in the ceremony and contemporary music at the party, and you could have two cakes at the reception—one white and one chocolate.
Bob: Sounds OK to me.
Cheryl: Me, too.
Bob: Hey! We did it!
Cheryl: Yeah! I'm so happy.
Marie: Excuse me.
Cheryl: Oh, Marie, thank you so much.
Bob: You're amazing! We couldn't have done it without you.

Scene 2

Paul: Hi. Lunchtime is over. Are you coming up to the office?
Bob: I'm too tired to go back to the office. Planning a wedding is hard work. I need a holiday.
Paul: Let's make today a holiday. We'll tell Mr. Evans we can't come back to work.
Bob: That's a great idea.
Marie: What are we celebrating?
Paul: You're getting married. How about National Wedding Day?
Bob: What happens on National Wedding Day?
Paul: I don't know. Why am I the one who has to think of everything?
Marie: Why don't we make it National Singles Day instead? All the married people give gifts to their single friends.
Bob: No. Buying gifts is hard work. I want to enjoy myself on our new holiday.
Cheryl: What about a Red Day? Everybody wears red clothes, and there's dancing in the street that goes on all night.
Bob: How about National Buy-Your-Friend-Another-Cup-of-Coffee Day?
Paul: Nice try.
Mr. Evans: How about National On-Time Day?
Bob: What happens on National On-Time Day?
Mr. Evans: You remind one another to come back to work on time.
Paul: Happy holiday.
Mr. Evans: Waitress!

On-the-Street Interviews

Interviewer: You're from Germany. What is a wedding like in Germany?
Jessica: Well, first of all, you have to have a civil ceremony where you go to the City Hall, and . . . well, you make everything official. And then traditionally, you go to church and have the religious ceremony.

Interviewer: And is there a wedding reception afterwards?
Jessica: Usually there is, of course. After church when everybody's waiting for the broom and the bride coming out and throwing rice at them and flowers, and then the whole crew's going to a nice place and having dinner and having a party.
Interviewer: You mentioned that your family is originally from Ghana.
Emma: Yes.
Interviewer: Could you tell me a little bit about the courtship and marriage ceremonies of your country?
Emma: There's a traditional . . . sometimes they do involve, like the American type of wedding, the very traditional. You walk down the aisle. But they also, there's also the traditional part in African culture. You wear the clothing and the outfits. It's much longer. Sometimes it can go into the next day. Some people extend.
Interviewer: Tell me about the reception.
Emma: They find a place to go to, or it's outside sometimes, there's a big tent. It just depends on the bride and groom, what they want. And there's tons of dancing, traditional dancing, eating, lots of food. Sometimes you have somebody come in and talk about how they know him and how good he is and what he's done and, you know, people giving lots of wisdom of how to be together. It's just . . . it's just really a great thing.

Unit 6

Sitcom

Scene 1

Mr. Evans: So, Mrs. Beatty, you're looking for an exciting place for your next vacation.
Mrs. Beatty: I usually travel to major cities in Europe, but this time I want to go someplace different—someplace away from the city—as long as it's safe.
Mr. Evans: How about California? The Big Sur area is spectacular.
Mrs. Beatty: California has lots of earthquakes, doesn't it?
Mr. Evans: Well, they have earthquakes occasionally. But not very often.
Mrs. Beatty: But it *does* have earthquakes.
Mr. Evans: Yes.
Mrs. Beatty: I'm not going.
Mr. Evans: OK. How about someplace in Asia? A beach in Thailand? Ko Chang has beautiful beaches, and it's very quiet there.
Mrs. Beatty: A quiet beach sounds nice. But they said on the news there's a monsoon in Thailand.
Mr. Evans: But the monsoon will be over by the time you go.
Mrs. Beatty: What else can you recommend?
Mr. Evans: Australia. The Australian outback is amazing.
Mrs. Beatty: I've heard they have tornadoes in Australia.
Mr. Evans: Well, some parts . . .
Mrs. Beatty: Where else?
Mr. Evans: Jamaica?
Mrs. Beatty: Hurricanes.
Mr. Evans: South Africa?
Mrs. Beatty: Floods.
Mr. Evans: Hawaii?
Mrs. Beatty: Landslides.
Mr. Evans: You know a lot about natural disasters, don't you, Mrs. Beatty? Let's see. What about Finland?
Mrs. Beatty: Finland?
Mr. Evans: It's wild, beautiful, and very different from other parts of Europe. And nothing bad ever happens in Finland.
Mrs. Beatty: Finland sounds good. I'll go to Finland.
Mr. Evans: Great. I'll book your tickets.

Scene 2

Mr. Evans: OK, I just booked your tickets to Helsinki, Finland. You'll be staying at the Palace Hotel.
Mrs. Beatty: That's great.
Marie: Excuse me, Mr. Evans?
Mr. Evans: Yes, Marie?
Marie: Mr. Woods is on the phone. He told me to tell you it's urgent.
Mr. Evans: Urgent?
Marie: He's traveling, you know.
Mr. Evans: Yes?
Marie: He said there's some kind of epidemic.
Mr. Evans: What kind of epidemic?
Marie: It sounds like it's that new influenza.
Mr. Evans: But he was vaccinated for that before he left.
Marie: I know. But he told me to tell you that he wants to fly home today.
Mr. Evans: On the Internet it says only three people are sick. That is not an epidemic. And it's not like anybody is dying from this flu.
Marie: He said he didn't want to be the first.
Mrs. Beatty: Where is he traveling, may I ask?
Marie: He's in Finland.
Mrs. Beatty: Finland? I just booked tickets to Finland!
Mr. Evans: Mrs. Beatty, everything will be fine. You'll get vaccinated, and you'll have nothing to worry about.
Mrs. Beatty: I'm not going to Finland. You told me nothing bad ever happens in Finland.
Mr. Evans: Mrs. Beatty, I can't think of anywhere in the world you can go and be completely safe. Right here in this city you could go outside and get hit by a bus. But you can't let that stop you from doing the things you want to do. Look. Why don't we go to lunch and we'll talk it over?
Marie: I don't think she's going anywhere.

Unit 7

Sitcom

Scene 1
Mr. Evans: Hello, Bob. Dining alone?
Bob: Paul and Marie went to get newspapers.
Mr. Evans: Do you mind if I join you?
Bob: Please, sit down.
Mr. Evans: May I ask what you're reading?
Bob: Um . . . *A History of the World.*
Mr. Evans: The bestseller? I'm very impressed! Reading nonfiction over lunch! I hear *that it's a very difficult book.*
Bob: Oh . . . uh, no. It's a pretty easy read. I . . . I can't put it down, actually.
Mr. Evans: A real page-turner, huh? Do you think I could borrow it when you're done?
Bob: Sure.
Mr. Evans: I usually prefer fiction myself. You know, thrillers, mysteries . . . There's nothing like curling up with a good science-fiction novel, is there?
Bob: You read science fiction, too?
Mr. Evans: Don't tell anyone. Are you learning a lot from your book?
Bob: Uh, yes. I think so.
Mr. Evans: So tell me what you're reading about right now.
Bob: Um . . . this part is about Great Britain.
Mr. Evans: Really? Do you mind if I take a look?
Bob: Cheryl hates when I read comics.
Mr. Evans: Then I can understand why you can't put the book down. Do you think that I could borrow it, then?
Bob: I'm still reading this one, but I have another one I can loan you.
Mr. Evans: I meant this one.
Bob: Oh, help yourself.

Scene 2
Paul: Look at this. The paper says that a tornado carried a woman for 300 miles, and she lived to tell about it.
Marie: I'm not sure if you know this, but that story isn't true.
Paul: It's in the paper. It must be true.
Marie: That paper is trash. I can't believe you're reading it.
Paul: What do you mean?
Marie: It's fiction, not news. Nothing in there is true. If you want real news, you have to read this paper.
Paul: That paper is boring. This one's much more interesting.
Marie: "Woman Gives Birth to Cow!" "Man Builds House from Bread!" "Baby with Two Heads!" Come on. This is offensive.
Paul: "Storm Kills 100 in Texas." "Train Accident Kills Five, Injures More." "Man Kills Wife and Son." I'm sorry, but all that death and destruction is pretty offensive to me.
Marie: I know that these things happened. And I know that those didn't.
Paul: You don't know that. You just assume that it's true.
Marie: Let's ask Bob and Mr. Evans what paper they read. Never mind. Let's just read.
Paul: That sounds good to me. Look at this! "A Man with Four Legs!"

On-the-Street Interviews
Interviewer: Do you folks do a lot of reading?
Herb: She does.
Blanche: I do, particularly. I like to read novels and mystery stories, sometimes travel stories.
Interviewer: Do you buy books, or do you get them from the library?
Lorayn: I buy books, and I tend to trade them with friends.
Interviewer: How about books on tape?
Blanche: I tried that. They put me to sleep.
Interviewer: So, novels. You like to read fiction. What are some of your favorite authors?
Dan: I just read Nick Hornby—*How to Be Good*—which was probably the funniest book I've ever read.
Interviewer: Would you say it's a real page-turner?
Dan: Absolutely. Absolutely. I mean, belly laughs on every page.
Interviewer: So, do you read anything else like newspapers, magazines?
Alvino: I do read magazines, yes.
Interviewer: Could you tell me, let's see, what sorts of magazines you like to read?
Alvino: Fashion. I enjoy fashion—*Details*, actually.
Interviewer: How about how-to magazines? Do you ever buy magazines about home repair or cooking, for instance?
Lorayn: I buy my husband magazines on . . . how-to magazines. He's the one that's good at fixing things and repair, even cooking.
Interviewer: How about newspapers? Do you read newspapers?
Dan: The *New York Times* when I'm home.
Interviewer: And what part of the newspapers are most important to you?
Dan: The front page and "Arts and Leisure."

Unit 8

Sitcom

Scene 1
Marie: What are those wacky glasses you are wearing?
Bob: These are ultra high-tech, top-of-the-line, state-of-the-art, cutting-edge TV glasses.
Marie: And you're actually watching TV right now?
Bob: Yeah. Right here on the corner.

Marie: What are you watching?
Bob: The basketball game.
Marie: Unbelievable. And Cheryl doesn't mind this?
Bob: Yes!!
Marie: What?!
Bob: Sorry. My team's winning.
Marie: This new invention doesn't bother you?
Cheryl: Are you kidding? If I had known how happy they would make him, I would have bought those glasses for Bob long ago.
Marie: Technology today is amazing. You know, I wish they'd invent something that would make people who talk on cell phones quieter. This guy in the café today was so loud, I couldn't hear myself talking.
Bob: Ha-Ha-Ha . . .
Marie: It wasn't funny.
Bob: What? Oh, sorry. I was laughing at this guy on TV.
Cheryl: If I could invent something, it would be a thing for Bob's car that would automatically charge him when he goes over the speed limit. He drives so fast sometimes, but he'd slow down if he had to pay.
Bob: No!
Marie: Is your team losing?
Bob: No. I heard what you said. You just leave my car alone.

Scene 2
Cheryl: Hi, Paul.
Paul: Wait 'til you see what I've got.
Bob: What is it?
Paul: Well, I have this problem with my cell phone. Whenever I'm traveling with a group, I can never hear it ring or feel it vibrate. So I got this thing that lets me know whenever my phone is ringing.
Marie: How does it do that?
Paul: It buzzes me.
Marie: Buzzes?
Paul: You know, bzzz, bzzz. So I can feel it.
Cheryl: Does it work?
Paul: I don't know. No one has called me yet . . . Ow!
Marie: What?!
Paul: Someone's calling me! Hello? Hello? No one's there. Wow. That was a big buzz. That almost hurt.
Cheryl: Maybe it isn't working right.
Paul: It's working fine . . . Ooh! Ow! Another phone call. Hello? Hello? That's strange. Man, if I ever get used to that, I'll always know whenever my phone is ringing . . . Ahhhhhhh! Stop calling me!
Marie: Paul. If I were you, I would take that thing back to the store before you hurt yourself.
Paul: I'm going. I'll see you later.
Marie: I hope he can drive OK.
Bob: He'll be fine.
Cheryl: How do you know?
Bob: I'll stop calling him.

Unit 9
Sitcom
Scene 1
Paul: Did you see the politicians expect to raise taxes again?
Bob: Really? What has the government decided to spend our money on now?
Paul: They're planning to build a stronger military.
Marie: It's wrong to spend so much on the military. They should spend it on education instead.
Cheryl: Can we please avoid discussing politics?
Marie: Why?
Cheryl: Every time we begin talking about politics, people get mad at each other.
Bob: They should spend more money on fighting corruption. If they were able to stop corrupt officials, maybe they wouldn't need to raise our taxes.
Paul: That's true, but I think we need to spend more money on the military. Without a strong military, the world won't be very safe.
Marie: That's one way to look at it. But maybe the world would be safer—and better—if we tried to eliminate poverty.
Bob: What do you think, Cheryl?
Cheryl: I think that if I say what I really think, you'll get all mad and call me crazy or ridiculous.
Marie: Cheryl. Don't be so afraid. We're only talking.
Cheryl: I think that the government should spend more money on cooking schools.
Marie: What?
Cheryl: Most people don't know how to cook well. I think the government should help teach them.
Marie: That's ridiculous!
Bob: Are you crazy?
Paul: Use our taxes to pay for cooking schools?
Cheryl: Of course not! But look at you. You're all mad at me. This is why I never discuss politics with friends. But don't let me stop you from getting mad at each other.

Scene 2
Marie: Paul, I never knew you were so conservative.
Paul: I'm not conservative.
Marie: Sure you are. You always seem to want things to be just like they used to be.
Paul: That's not conservative. That's just smart. (to Cheryl) Thanks.
Marie: That's the definition of conservative.
Paul: Really? Well, I didn't know you were so radical.
Marie: What makes you think I'm radical?
Paul: You always want to change everything.
Marie: No, I don't. I just want our government to realize that it's the twenty-first century and they need new ways of doing things. (to Cheryl) Thank you.
Paul: That sounds radical to me.

Marie: Bob, tell him I'm not a radical.
Bob: She's not a radical. She's a liberal. Like me.
Marie: I wouldn't call you a liberal.
Bob: Oh, really?
Marie: I'd say you're more of a moderate. You're always in the middle.
Bob: If I want to be a liberal, I'll be a liberal. *(to Cheryl)* Thank you, honey.
Marie: You can be whatever you want, you just can't be one thing and call it something else.
Paul: Listen to you. You're like a little dictator.
Marie: I studied politics in school. I know something about the definitions of political beliefs.
Paul: Is that so? So what is Cheryl? A radical? Moderate? Conservative?
Marie: Who knows? She's not saying.
Paul: Cheryl, what are you? Would you mind telling us that much?
Cheryl: OK. You want to know what I believe? I believe . . . I believe . . . I believe these are the best chips I have ever tasted.

On-the-Street Interviews

Interviewer: How do you feel about prohibiting smoking indoors?
Ian: As a smoker I don't appreciate it all the time, but I can understand why.
Christiane: I think it's fantastic. I think it's great. If you go to restaurants and nobody can smoke, the food tastes better and your clothes don't smell.
Interviewer: How about censorship of books or movies by a government?
Stephan: I am 100 percent against censorship of any books or movies or any expression of creativity, and I feel that when governments try to censor books or movies, then it creates a sort of atmosphere of fear, and people don't get to . . . don't have ready access to information that should be available to them.
Interviewer: If you could tell me maybe two things that you think are big problems in the world today . . .
Christiane: I think one of the biggest problems is war. And I think another big problem is racism in this world.
Interviewer: And of those, could you tell me, you know, a little bit more about what you think could be done to alleviate these problems?
Christiane: I think, actually with both problems, it's mostly about understanding each other and sitting down on a table and . . . talk, get to know each other and be able to make more compromises and understand different cultures and reasons why people do certain things certain ways. And I think we would all be much happier.
Interviewer: Communication.
Christiane: Communication. That's the clue. Exactly. Yeah.

Unit 10

Sitcom

Scene 1

Cheryl: Everyone, we'd like to ask your opinion about something.
Mr. Evans: What is that?
Cheryl: We're trying to decide where to go on vacation after the wedding, for our honeymoon.
Bob: We thought you might be able to help us decide on a location.
Mr. Evans: An excellent idea. Where are you thinking of going?
Cheryl: Well, Bob doesn't really like to travel, so he's agreed to go wherever I want to go, as long as the hotel has nice bathrooms and a TV.
Mr. Evans: That sounds fair. What's your first choice?
Cheryl: I've always wanted to go to Cozumel, off the Yucatan Peninsula.
Paul: Cozumel is spectacular. The island itself is pretty flat, but the beaches are beautiful, and the ocean is so blue.
Marie: Aren't there too many sharks to go swimming there?
Paul: No! It's very safe. What? Oh! But it's somewhat overrated.
Bob: You just said . . .
Mr. Evans: What else are you thinking of?
Cheryl: What about Tierra del Fuego in the south of Argentina and Chile?
Paul: The scenery is extraordinary! The mountain ranges and national parks are breathtaking.
Marie: But in June won't it be too dark to do very much?
Paul: No! Plenty of people go there in June to go skiing or . . . But, of course, it's probably not romantic enough for a honeymoon.
Cheryl: I've heard the jungles and rain forests in Malaysia are a must-see.
Paul: They're so lush . . . Of course, some people feel that the scorpions make it too dangerous to hike.
Bob: We could go to that hotel on Grant Street along the river.
Cheryl: Stay in town? For our honeymoon?
Bob: Well, I heard the rooms have really nice bathrooms and big televisions.

Scene 2

Marie: Cheryl, you once told me that you wanted to go to Tahiti.
Cheryl: That's right. I forgot about that.
Mr. Evans: You would love Tahiti.
Paul: One of the most beautiful places on earth.
Marie: And very, very romantic.
Cheryl: Really? You all think Tahiti is a good idea?
Mr. Evans: I think you'd love it.
Bob: It's too expensive.
Cheryl: How expensive?

Bob: Well, do you remember how much Mr. Rashid's vacation to Tahiti cost?
Cheryl: Yes, I do.
Bob: He traveled cheaply.
Cheryl: Well, that's it. I'm out of ideas. I guess we'll go someplace boring.
Mr. Evans: We weren't going to tell you until a couple of months from now, but Paul, Marie, and I were talking, and we thought a vacation in the South Pacific would be perfect.
Cheryl: I just wish we could afford it.
Mr. Evans: So we decided that as our wedding gift to you, we would like to send you to Tahiti. All expenses paid.
Cheryl: You're kidding!
Mr. Evans: We've booked your flights and a hotel on the southern coast for two weeks.
Cheryl: I don't know how to thank you!
Bob: But the . . .
Mr. Evans: And the hotel room has a spectacular bathroom and a TV this big.
Bob: I don't know how to thank you!
Cheryl: Thank you so much! I'm so excited!

Top Notch Pop
Lyrics

Top Notch Pop Lyrics

It's a Great Day for Love [Unit 1]

Wherever you go,
there are things you should know,
so be aware
of the customs and views—
all the do's and taboos—
of people there.
You were just a stranger in a sea of new faces.
Now we're **making small talk**[1] on a first-name basis.

It's a great day for love, isn't it?
Aren't you the one I was hoping to find?
It's a great day for love, isn't it?
By the time you said hello,
I had already made up my mind.

Wherever you stay
be sure to obey
the golden rules[2],
and before you relax,
brush up on the facts[3]
you learned at school.
Try to be polite and always be sure to get
some friendly advice on proper etiquette.

It's a great day for love, isn't it?
Aren't you the one I was hoping to find?
It's a great day for love, isn't it?
By the time you said hello,
I had already made up my mind.

And when you smiled at me
and I fell in love,
the sun had just appeared
in the sky above.
You know how much I care, don't you?
And you'll always be there, won't you?

It's a great day for love, isn't it?
Aren't you the one I was hoping to find?
It's a great day for love, isn't it?
By the time you said hello,
I had already made up my mind.

LANGUAGE NOTES
[1] **making small talk** = chatting about general topics such as the weather, work, preferences, family, etc.
[2] **the golden rules** = an old-fashioned way to refer to the kinds of rules for behavior and character one learns as a child in school
[3] **brush up on something** = try to remember what one has learned previously but may have forgotten

I'll Get Back to You [Unit 3]

Your camera isn't working right.
It needs a few repairs.
You make me **ship it**[1] overnight.
Nothing else compares.
You had to lengthen your new skirt,
and now you want to get
someone to wash your fancy shirts
and dry them when they're wet.
Come a little closer—
let me whisper in your ear.
Is my message getting across[2]
to you **loud and clear**[3]?

You're always making plans.
I'll tell you what I'll do:
let me **think it over**[4] and
I'll get back to you[5].
You want to get your suit dry-cleaned.
You want to get someone
to shorten your new pair of jeans
and call you when they're done.
I guess I'll have them print a sign
and hang it on your shelf,
with four small words in one big line:
"Just do it yourself."
Let me tell you what this song
is really all about.
I'm getting tired of waiting while you
figure it out[6].
I've heard all your demands,
but I have a life, too.
Let me think it over and
I'll get back to you.
I'm really reliable,
incredibly fast,
extremely helpful

from first to last.
Let me see what I can do.
Day after day,
everybody knows
I always do what I say.

You're always making plans.
I'll tell you what I'll do:
let me think it over and
I'll get back to you.

> **LANGUAGE NOTES**
> [1] **ship something** = send it
> [2] **get something across to someone** = make someone understand something
> [3] **loud and clear** = very clear
> [4] **think something over** = think carefully about something
> [5] **get back to someone** = call that person again in order to give him or her information he or she requested
> [6] **figure something out** = begin to understand something

Endless Holiday [Unit 5]

Day after day,
all my thoughts drift away
before they've begun.
I sit in my room
in the darkness and **gloom**[1]
just waiting for someone
to take me to a tourist town,
with parties in the street and people dancing to a joyful sound.

It's a song that people sing.
It's the laughter that you bring
on an endless holiday.
It's the happiness inside.
It's a roller coaster ride
on an endless holiday.

I try and I try
to work hard, but I
get lost in **a daze**[2],
and I think about
how sad life is without
a few good holidays.
I close my eyes, pull down the **shade**[3],
and in my imagination I am dancing in a big parade,

and the music is loud.
I get lost in the crowd
on an endless holiday.
It's a picnic at noon.
It's a trip to the moon
on an endless holiday,
with flags and **confetti**[4],
wild costumes and a great big marching band,
as we wish each other well
in a language we all understand.
The sky above fills with the light
of fireworks exploding, as we dance along the street tonight.

It's a song that people sing.
It's the laughter that you bring
on an endless holiday.
It's the happiness inside.
It's a roller coaster ride
on an endless holiday.

> **LANGUAGE NOTES**
> [1] **gloom** = unhappiness
> [2] **a daze** = a state of confusion
> [3] **a shade** = a covering for a window
> [4] **confetti** = tiny pieces of colorful paper that are sometimes thrown during parades or other street celebrations

Lucky to Be Alive [Unit 6]

Thank you for helping me to survive.
I'm really lucky to be alive.

When I was caught in a freezing snowstorm,
you taught me how to stay warm.
When I was running from a landslide
with no place to hide,
you protected me from injury.
Even the world's biggest tsunami
has **got nothing on me**[1],
because you can go faster.
You keep me safe from disaster.
You're like some kind of hero—
you're the best friend that I know.

Thank you for helping me to survive.
I'm really lucky to be alive.

When the big flood came with the pouring rain,
they were saying that a natural disaster loomed.
You just opened your umbrella.
You were the only fellow who kept calm and prepared.
You found us shelter.
I never felt like anybody cared
the way that you did when you said,
"I will always be there—
you can bet your life on it."
And when the cyclone turned the day into night,
you held a flashlight and showed me the safe way home.
You called for help on your cell phone.
You said you'd never leave me.
You said, "Believe me,
in times of trouble you will never be alone."
They said it wasn't such a bad situation.
It was **beyond imagination**[2].
I'm just glad to be alive—
and that is no exaggeration.

Thank you for helping me to survive.
I'm really lucky to be alive.

> **LANGUAGE NOTES**
> [1] **got nothing on me** = can't hurt me
> [2] **beyond imagination** = really terrible

Reinvent the Wheel[1] [Unit 8]

You've got your digi camera with the Powershot,
Four mega pixels and a memory slot.
You've got your e-mail and your Internet.
You send me pictures of your digi pet.
I got the digi dog and the digi cat,
the digi this and the digi that.
I hate to be the one to **break the news**[2],
but you're giving me the digi blues,

And you don't know
the way I really feel.
Why'd you have to go and
reinvent the wheel?

You've got your cordless phone and your microwave,
and your Reflex Plus for the perfect shave.
It's super special, top of the line,
with the latest new, cutting-edge design.

You've got your SLR and your LCD,
your PS2 and your USB.
I've seen the future and it's pretty grim:
they've used up all the acronyms.

And you don't know
the way I really feel.
Why'd you have to go and
reinvent the wheel?

I keep waiting for a breakthrough innovation:
something to help our poor communication.
Hey, where'd you get all of that high-tech taste?
Your faith in progress is such a waste.
Your life may be state of the art,
but you don't understand the human heart.

And you don't know
the way I really feel.
Why'd you have to go and
reinvent the wheel?

> **LANGUAGE NOTES**
> [1] **reinvent the wheel** = to unnecessarily re-do something that's already been done
> [2] **break the news** = be the first to tell

Answer Key

Answer Key

Unit 1

Preview
A.
1. a 2. a 3. b 4. a 5. b
B.
1. first 2. Ms. 3. Of course not 4. formal

Sitcom

Scene 1
A.
her name, the weather, her nationality
B.
1. aren't 2. aren't 3. are 4. isn't
C.
1. b 2. c 3. b 4. b
D.
1. won't you 2. isn't he 3. aren't we 4. aren't they 5. is he 6. did she 7. won't you 8. shouldn't they 9. would they 10. can't you

Scene 2
A.
using proper greetings; pointing; using hand gestures to say, "Come with me"; knowing how close to stand next to someone
B.
1. b 2. a 3. b 4. b 5. b
C.
Answers will vary but should include variations on the following:
1. If Mr. Rashid had been a woman, he would have insulted her. Men and women do not touch in India.
2. His gesture means "Go away." 3. He stands too close to Mr. Rashid. 4. He should bow and say, "Namaste."
5. The way he points is a rude gesture in India.
D.
1. Women and men, do not touch 2. to go away 3. too close, this far away 4. Do it like this 5. Pointing with your fingers, Use your chin
G.
1. had already decided 2. had asked 3. had already used 4. had insulted 5. had done 6. had made

Top Notch Pop Song
A.
1. a 2. a
B.
Be aware of people's customs, Obey the rules wherever you go, Remember anything you've ever studied about places you visit, Ask for etiquette advice

C.
1. It's a great day for love, isn't it? 2. Aren't you the one I was hoping to find? 3. You know how much I care, don't you? 4. And you'll always be there, won't you?

Unit 2

Preview
A.
1. F 2. F 3. F 4. T 5. T 6. F 7. F 8. F
C.
1. must 2. must 3. must not

Sitcom

Scene 1
A.
1. may be stopping by 2. may have to go 3. must get 4. might help 5. may be able to help 6. might prefer
B.
1. a 2. b 3. a 4. c 5. a 6. c
C.
1. F 2. F 3. T 4. F 5. F 6. T
E.
Answers will vary but may include the following:
2. A painkiller might help. 3. You might want to go to a chiropractor. 4. You may have to go to a doctor. 5. An antacid might make you feel better.

Scene 2
A.
painkillers, cold tablets, nasal spray, cough medicines, vitamins, antacids, decongestants
B.
1. Dr. Anderson 2. Paul 3. Cheryl 4. Dr. Anderson 5. Paul 6. Bob 7. Marie
C.
1. a 2. a 3. b 4. a 5. b 6. c
D.
Answers will vary but may include the following:
Dr. Anderson asks Paul what medicine he has taken. Paul lists cough medicine, vitamins, antacid, and a decongestant. He also says that his friend Don has had a cold all week. Paul also started a new exercise routine last night. Dr. Anderson says that he took too much medicine and that he exercised too much.

On-the-Street-Interviews
A.
1. a 2. c 3. c 4. b 5. c

B.
1. believe in Western medicine, nontraditional treatments, acupuncture or homeopathic medicine
2. what are the advantages, medicine and surgery
3. disadvantages of Western medicine
4. nontraditional therapies that you use

Unit 3

Preview

A.
1. have / get my suit cleaned 2. have / get my car repainted 3. have / get 200 color documents copied 4. have / get a package sent 5. have / get our plane tickets delivered

B.
1. Why don't you have your assistant make a reservation at the restaurant? 2. I'm going to have the tour guide explain how to get there. 3. She had her husband pick up the package at the airport last week. 4. At our wedding last year, we had the chef prepare a special dish for our guests. 5. You can have the tour bus meet the group in front of the bus station.

C.
2. …have those color prints made 3. …get my house cleaned … 4. …had our car repaired … 5. …have my secretary make some coffee … 6. …got the copier repaired … 7. …have your assistant call …

Sitcom

Scene 1

A.
1. Marie 2. Paul 3. Cheryl 4. Bob 5. Mr. Evans

B.
1. Mr. Evans, Mr. Rashid 2. Mr. Wells, the day after tomorrow 3. National Express, Australia 4. Cheryl, Harper's 5. Mr. Evans, a tailor

C.
1. had everything mailed to them 2. we gave you the package, to give to Mr. Wells 3. have them reprint 4. get twenty-five color documents printed

Scene 2

A.
1. a 2. e 3. c 4. b 5. d

B.
1. F 2. F 3. F 4. T 5. NI 6. T 7. NI 8. F

C.
1. have you choose 2. had them give 3. had the restaurant put

D.
1. let 2. gets 3. makes 4. lets 5. gets 6. makes

Top Notch Pop Song

A.
1. make me ship it 2. lengthen your new skirt 3. get 4. wash 5. dry them 6. get your suit dry-cleaned 7. get 8. shorten 9. call 10. have them print

B.
1. She wanted to get it lengthened. 2. She wants to get them washed and dried when they're wet. 3. He wants to get his suit dry-cleaned and his jeans shortened. 4. Just do it yourself.

Unit 4

Preview

A.
1. she was going to / would get married at age 18
2. she wasn't going to / wouldn't get married 3. he was going to / would be an astronaut

Sitcom

Scene 1

A.
1. was going to be 2. thought I would, have to work, was afraid, would, meet 3. was going to be 4. was going to be

B.
1. c 2. c 3. a 4. b 5. c

C.
Answers will vary but should include variations on the following:
1. She thought she was going to be a chef. 2. Her mother talked her out of it. 3. She thought Cheryl would always have to work at night and would never get married. 4. Before he met Cheryl, Bob ate only fast food. 5. The diet was too hard.

Scene 2

A.
He's very polite, he knows which fork to use, he knows the customs of other cultures.

B.
1. What did you think you were going to be 2. I always thought I would have 3. would have made 4. about the customs of other cultures

C.
1. Marie 2. Cheryl 3. Paul 4. Bob 5. Cheryl

D.
2. Mr. Evans gives a speech … 3. …program is *International Etiquette with Evans*. 4. …hopes the others won't laugh … 5. Mr. Evans has always been interested …

B.
Answers will vary but may include the following: a parade, flags and confetti, loud music, wild costumes, a crowd, a big marching band, a picnic, fireworks

Unit 6

Preview
A.
1. a drought 2. A landslide 3. earthquake
4. A tornado 5. an epidemic 6. a flood
7. A hurricane / typhoon / monsoon

Sitcom
Scene 1
A.
1. a 2. b 3. a 4. d 5. c
B.
1. b 2. b 3. a 4. b 5. a 6. b 7. a
C.
1. T 2. F 3. F 4. T 5. T 6. F

Scene 2
A.
1. booked your tickets, 'll be staying, That's great
2. Excuse me, is on the phone, urgent 3. epidemic, What kind of epidemic, It sounds like 4. told me to tell you, says only three people
B.
1. b 2. b 3. b 4. b 5. c
C.
1. Marie has a message… 2. Mr. Woods is calling Mr. Evans. 3. …wants to fly home. 4. Mr. Woods was vaccinated… 5. Three people… 6. …Mrs. Beatty can get vaccinated. 7. …she doesn't want to go to Finland.
D.
Answers will vary but should include variations on the following:
Mr. Evans had booked tickets for Mrs. Beatty to fly to Finland. But then Mr. Woods called to say that he wanted to fly home from Finland, because there was an epidemic there. Even though only three people were sick, Mrs. Beatty changed her mind and decided not to go to Finland.
E.
1. said 2. was 3. say 4. told 5. to forget 6. said
7. there had been 8. told 9. told 10. wanted
11. tell 12. said 13. not to worry
F.
1. to go to Puerto Rico for a beautiful beach vacation.
2. he usually traveled to major cities in the United States.
3. would call me tomorrow. 4. we weren't going to Europe this year. 5. a quiet beach sounded nice.

G.
Answers will vary but should include variations on the following:
1. She told him that Mr. Woods was on the phone.
2. He told her to tell Mr. Evans that he wanted to fly home. 3. He said there was an epidemic in Finland.
4. It said that only three people were sick. 5. She said she wasn't going to Finland.

Top Notch Pop Song
A.
1. landslide 2. tsunami 3. disaster 4. flood 5. rain
6. natural disaster 7. who kept calm and prepared
8. I will always be there 9. showed me the safe way home 10. You said you'd never leave me 11. You said, "Believe me, 12. you will never be alone 13. it wasn't such a bad situation 14. I'm just glad to be alive
B.
1. Expressing gratitude to a friend who helped him survive various disasters and how lucky he feels to be alive.
2. **a.** The friend taught him how to stay warm.
   b. The friend protected him from injury.
   c. The friend found them shelter.
   d. The friend held a flashlight, showed him the safe way home, and called for help on a cell phone.
3. He's thankful for the friend's help and for being alive.

Unit 7

Preview
A.
1. k 2. e 3. h 4. c 5. g 6. b
B.
1. if / whether he likes to read a lot? 2. where she bought that new novel. 3. if / whether he prefers reading mysteries or thrillers. 4. why you read so many comic books. 5. who collected these short stories.
6. when he started writing his autobiography?

Sitcom
Scene 1
A.
fiction, mysteries, thrillers, science fiction
B.
1. b 2. a 3. c 4. b 5. a
C.
1. what you're reading 2. I could borrow it when you're done 3. what you're reading about right now 4. if I take a look
D.
1. page-turner 2. hard to follow 3. fast read 4. trash
5. cliffhanger 6. bestseller

On-the-Street-Interviews

A.
1. F Rita is an elementary school teacher. 2. F San would like to be a television producer. 3. T 4. F San is good at art. 5. T

B.
1. a 2. c 3. b 4. c

C.
1. what your career or occupation is, school teacher, career, will be, I work in television, I would like to
2. think that you'd be in marketing, I thought I'd be, drive a 3. a good career for you, I love children, the idea of, knowledge 4. What would you say, I have a lot of artistic ability, skills and talents 5. talents and abilities, they're a combination

Unit 5

Preview

A.
1. engaged 2. bride 3. guests 4. wedding ceremony 5. reception 6. traditional 7. groom 8. newlyweds 9. honeymoon

Sitcom

Scene 1

A.

	Bob
The number of guests	20
The location of the ceremony	park or beach
The type of music at the ceremony	contemporary
The length of the ceremony	short
The length of the reception	long
The type of wedding cake	chocolate

	Cheryl
The number of guests	300
The location of the ceremony	indoors
The type of music at the ceremony	traditional
The length of the ceremony	long
The length of the reception	short
The type of wedding cake	white

B.
1. b 2. a 3. c 4. a 5. b 6. b

C.

The size of the wedding	Plan a big wedding
The location of the ceremony	the park on Oak Street
The type of music at the ceremony	traditional
The type of music at the reception	contemporary
The type of wedding cake	two cakes—one white and one chocolate

D.
1. that (wedding) 2. that (dress) 3. who (relatives) 4. that (band) 5. who (woman)

E.
1. that is very beautiful 2. that can hold a lot of people 3. who catches the bouquet of flowers 4. the groom chooses 5. that combines traditional and contemporary features 6. I work with at my company 7. her mother wore 8. their colleagues paid for

Scene 2

A.
1. c 2. a 3. d 4. e 5. b

B.
National Singles Day: All the married people give gifts to their single friends.
Red Day: Everybody wears red clothes, and there's dancing in the street.
National On-Time Day: People remind one another to come back to work on time.

C.
Answers will vary but should include variations on the following:
1. To tell the others that lunchtime is over. 2. He's too tired from planning the wedding. 3. Because Bob wants Paul to buy him the coffee. 4. He wants his employees to come back to work.

On-the-Street-Interviews

A.
1. b 2. c 3. c 4. c

B.
1. throwing rice at the bride and groom, a ceremony at City Hall, a ceremony at a church 2. walking down the aisle, wearing traditional African clothes, celebrating for more than one day

Top Notch Pop Song

A.
1. day 2. away 3. room 4. gloom 5. that people sing 6. that you bring 7. inside 8. ride 9. try 10. I 11. about 12. without 13. shade 14. parade 15. loud 16. crowd 17. picnic at noon 18. moon 19. costumes 20. wish each other well 21. understand 22. light 23. fireworks 24. tonight 25. that people sing 26. that you bring 27. happiness inside 28. roller coaster ride

Scene 2

A.
Baby with Two Heads, Woman Gives Birth to Cow, Man Builds House from Bread

B.
1. M **2.** M **3.** M **4.** P **5.** P **6.** M **7.** M

C.
1. fiction, offensive **2.** true, interesting **3.** offensive, boring

E.
1. (that) the stories in Paul's newspaper are offensive.
2. (that) the stories in his newspaper are all true.
3. (that) Bob and Mr. Evans would agree with her.
4. (that) a baby really had been born with two heads.
5. (that) Marie and Bob are never going to agree about this.

On-the-Street-Interviews

A.
newspapers, fashion magazines, how-to magazines, mysteries, travel books, novels, books on tape

B.
1. a **2.** b **3.** c **4.** c **5.** c

C.
2. F She says she buys books and trades them with friends. **3.** T She says books on tape put her to sleep. **4.** F Dan says it was a funny book. **5.** T The interviewer asks if he reads anything else. **6.** F She says that her husband is the one who is good at fixing things. **7.** F He says his favorite sections are the front page and "Arts and Leisure."

Unit 8

Preview

A.
1. a **2.** c **3.** c **4.** a **5.** b **6.** a **7.** b

B.
1. try **2.** can **3.** had known **4.** read **5.** would watch / could watch **6.** will spend **7.** would send

Sitcom

Scene 1

A.
1. F **2.** T **3.** T **4.** NI **5.** F **6.** T **7.** NI **8.** T **9.** F

B.
1. had known, would make, would have bought
2. they'd invent, would make **3.** could invent, would be, would charge, goes **4.** drives, he'd, if he had to

C.
Answers will vary but should include variations on the following:
1. That Bob is watching TV on them. **2.** He laughs at a man on TV. **3.** They make Bob happy. **4.** Because sometimes they're so loud that she can't hear herself talking. **5.** He would slow down.

Scene 2

A.
1. c **2.** a **3.** b **4.** a **5.** c

B.
1. whenever my phone is ringing **2.** get used to, I'll always know **3.** were you, would take **4.** I'll see you later. **5.** calling him

C.
1. Paul **2.** Marie **3.** Cheryl **4.** Bob

Top Notch Pop Song

A.
1. e-mail and your Internet **2.** You send me pictures
3. phone **4.** microwave **5.** top of the line
6. cutting-edge **7.** high-tech **8.** state of the art

B.
1. T **2.** T **3.** F **4.** F **5.** F

C.
1. poor communication **2.** He doesn't understand the human heart.

Unit 9

Preview

A.
1. terrorism **2.** corruption **3.** poverty
4. discrimination

B.
1. reactionary **2.** moderate **3.** conservative
4. liberal **5.** radical

Sitcom

Scene 1

A.
education, poverty, military spending, corruption

B.
1. Bob **2.** Marie **3.** Paul **4.** Cheryl

C.
Answers will vary but should include variations on the following:
1. Without a strong military, the world won't be very safe. **2.** If corruption is stopped, maybe they won't raise taxes. **3.** The world would be safer and better if we tried to eliminate poverty. **4.** Every time people talk about politics, they get mad at each other.

D.
1. crime, corruption **2.** poverty, is **3.** the candidate, education **4.** spending, health **5.** Discrimination, is, the world **6.** justice, terrorism

Scene 2

A.
1. doesn't think **2.** thinks **3.** doesn't think **4.** thinks
5. doesn't think **6.** thinks

B.
1. Marie, Paul 2. Paul, Marie 3. Marie, Bob 4. Marie, Bob 5. Marie, Bob 6. Paul, Marie 7. Marie, Cheryl

C.
Answers will vary but should include variations on the following:
1. it's the twenty-first century and they need new ways of doing things. 2. she studied politics in school. 3. these are the best chips she's ever tasted.

D.
2. The government needs to persuade drivers to wear their seat belts. 3. Restaurants shouldn't permit customers to smoke indoors. 4. People should urge the government to raise the voting age. 5. The university shouldn't allow the library staff to censor books. 6. Teachers should encourage students to participate in school affairs.

On-the-Street-Interviews

A.
1. Stephan 2. Christiane 3. Christiane 4. Ian

B.
1. a, b 2. b, c 3. a, d 4. a, b

C.
1. I can understand why 2. it's fantastic, it's great, the food tastes better, your clothes don't smell 3. censorship, any books or movies 4. mostly about understanding

---

Unit 10

Preview

A.
1. exhausting 2. steep 3. rocky 4. dark 5. slippery 6. dangerous 7. foggy

B.
1. too exhausting, to walk 2. too steep, too rocky to 3. too slippery, to walk 4. too foggy to see

Sitcom

Scene 1

A.
1. Cheryl, Bob 2. Mr. Evans 3. Bob 4. Cheryl 5. Paul 6. Marie 7. Paul 8. Cheryl 9. Paul 10. Paul 11. Cheryl 12. Paul

B.
1. a 2. c 3. c 4. a 5. a 6. c 7. c

C.
1. off the, spectacular, is pretty flat, beautiful, the ocean is so blue 2. too many sharks to go swimming there, it's somewhat overrated 3. extraordinary, breathtaking, too dark to do very much 4. are a must-see, so lush, scorpions make it too dangerous to hike

Scene 2

A.
1. Cheryl once told Marie … 2. Mr. Evans thinks Cheryl would love Tahiti. 3. Bob tells Cheryl … 4. …was very expensive. 5. Cheryl gives up because she's out … 6. Cheryl and Bob don't have to go … 7. …gives Cheryl and Bob a trip to Tahiti …

B.
1. a 2. a 3. b 4. c 5. b

C.
1. that you wanted to go to Tahiti, forgot about that 2. how much Mr. Rashid's vacation to Tahiti cost; Yes, I do; cheaply 3. out of ideas, we'll go someplace boring, weren't going to tell you, were talking, we thought, would be perfect 4. we would like to send you to Tahiti, You're kidding